English Heritage

Annual Report and Accounts 2011/2012

Presented to Parliament pursuant to Paragraph 13(4) of Schedule 3 to the National Heritage Act 1983

Ordered by the House of Commons to be printed on 11 July 2012

HC 266   London: The Stationery Office   £21.25

Any enquiries regarding this publication should be sent to us at:

Customer Services, English Heritage, The Engine House, Fire Fly Avenue, Swindon SN2 2EH
Telephone: 0870 333 1181
Fax: 01793 414926
Textphone: 01793 414878
Email: customers@english-heritage.org.uk

This document is available for download at www.official-documents.gov.uk. It is also available from our website at www.english-heritage.org.uk.

ISBN: 9780102976540

Printed in the UK for The Stationery Office Limited on behalf of the Controller of Her Majesty's Stationery Office.

ID 2486239 07/12

Printed on paper containing 100% recycled fibre content minimum

Product code: 51768

Contents

Introduction

This year has been uniquely challenging. We have faced a reduced budget and substantial internal restructuring whilst responding to the changes in the economic climate, local authorities and the planning system. Despite these odds however, I am delighted to say that it has been a very successful year: much has been done to inspire understanding and support for our heritage and the work that we do, opening up its possibilities to as many people as possible and making sure it will be enjoyed and valued for generations to come.

In the past year we have welcomed over 11 million visitors, attracted more members than ever before, opened exciting new sites and exhibitions, recognised the vital contribution of voluntary work through the Heritage Angel Awards, mobilised communities to the cause of industrial heritage helping to save Middleport Pottery and the Victoria Mill in Burnley in the process, engaged with local authorities and local bodies so that they can get the best out of their historic assets for the future, created the English Heritage Foundation, and done even more to raise the flag for heritage.

Our fundraising efforts have generated nearly £8 million. £2.5 million will go towards the improvements at Stonehenge for which we gained all necessary permissions this year. The works will enable visitors to enjoy the stones in a much improved setting, with greater access and world-class visitor facilities. We were delighted to be awarded funding from the Department for Education for the Heritage Schools Initiative; the £2.7 million over three years will be used to encourage teachers to use their local heritage in teaching the curriculum. We have also been able to complete the first phase of a 20-year restoration project at Wrest Park in Bedfordshire, after securing a £1.14 million Heritage Lottery Fund grant.

The National Heritage Protection Plan which launched in May 2011, underpins all our endeavours, setting out how we will work with partners in the sector, whilst using our resources in the most cost-effective way to promote sustainable development and thereby best protect England's vulnerable historic environment.

None of this could have been achieved without the unique knowledge and expertise of English Heritage staff who have faced the many challenges this year with resolution and professionalism. Their commitment to English Heritage shines through in the praise we consistently receive from the people we work with, from our members and from our visitors. I would like to thank them for their continuing hard work and unfailing support for the nation's heritage.

Baroness Andrews OBE
Chair

Chief Executive's Report

The protection of the historic environment rests in large part on the planning system which this year has been very substantially overhauled by Government. English Heritage is very pleased to have worked closely with Government on the National Planning Policy Framework (NPPF) and the Localism Act to secure a positive result for heritage and sustainable development. We believe that the level of protection that Planning Policy Statement 5 gave to heritage has been maintained in the NPPF. This will allow heritage to continue to play a central role in long-term sustainable growth in England. As there have been a number of changes to the wording we will of course want to monitor the outcome of planning decisions to ensure that the NPPF works in the way Government intends.

Its successful application will rely on expertise on the ground at a time when local authority staffing levels continue to decline. We understand local authority staff resources have fallen around 10% in the past year so this is a major cause for concern.

The consequence of the October 2010 Comprehensive Spending Review (CSR) was a cut in Grant in Aid for 2011/12 and further cuts in each of the following three years. If our spend and activity levels had remained unchanged, taking inflation into account, it would have given rise to an estimated budget deficit in 2011/12 of £20.1 million, rising to £51 million by 2014/15. We have taken various substantial steps to address this including restructuring, continued growth in commercial income, rationalising our grant-making and further efficiency and procurement savings. Our efforts kept us within budget for 2011/12 and we forecast a balanced budget for the next three years.

The National Heritage Protection Plan

The National Heritage Protection Plan aims to direct the understanding and articulation of the significance of the historic environment, as the key to its successful protection and management. English Heritage carries out some protection and management directly, for example, the part we play in defining significance for listing, our grant-giving, advice and guidance and in looking after the National Heritage Collection, while much protection and management is undertaken by others, particularly local authorities. We continue to work closely with the local planning authorities and successful collaborations this year have included the Lancashire Textile Mills project, the findings of which will be used to help owners and local authorities make informed development and planning decisions on surviving industrial heritage sites, while also identifying those which might be considered for listing.

One of the notable trends over the past year is the strengthening of links with the historic environment sector by working with them in new and more productive ways. By agreeing what can be carried out best by which partner, overall effectiveness and influence can be increased. One example of this is the National Heritage Protection Plan Advisory Board. With a membership from across the sector, the Board is increasingly influencing the National Heritage Protection Plan and indirectly, the priorities set by English Heritage.

The national coordination of Heritage Open Days returned to the voluntary sector this year after being in English Heritage's care temporarily after the demise of the Civic Trust. A consortia of The Heritage Alliance, Civic Voice and the National Trust took over England's largest grassroots heritage event on 1 October 2011. English Heritage continues to provide grant support and a staff member is on a temporary secondment to The Heritage Alliance to help the sector nurture philanthropic giving.

The rising cost of fuel and the challenge of tackling climate change continue to raise questions over the thermal efficiency of old buildings. We have a major research programme underway aimed at understanding the true performance of traditionally constructed buildings and the most effective means of meeting the twin objectives of improving insulation and conserving their importance to us.

Practical advice to owners, managers and professionals on how to conserve historic buildings can now be found in the first five volumes of the ten volume series, *Practical Building Conservation,* the suite of energy efficiency publications, *Energy Efficiency and Historic Buildings* and *The Maintenance and Repair of Traditional Farm Buildings: A Guide to Good Practice.*

Chief Executive's Report

Designation is one of the principal ways in which we identify, celebrate and protect our most important buildings and sites. In December, The Lloyd's Building in the City of London joined one of only around 9,000 buildings in England listed at Grade I, on English Heritage's recommendation. As a commercial building, Lloyd's is innovative; its futuristic high-tech design has a timelessness that makes it still appear ahead of its time 25 years after it opened. English Heritage worked closely with the owners at every stage of the listing process and a management agreement that identifies future options for change has been prepared. Its architect, Richard Rogers, was delighted at the listing. Also in December, Star Carr, the early Mesolithic occupation site near Scarborough in North Yorkshire, was made a scheduled monument for its rarity and archaeological importance. The designation provides legal protection for the site where last year a team of archaeologists from the Universities of York and Manchester discovered Britain's earliest surviving house which dates to at least 9,000 BC. Both these additions can be found on the National Heritage List for England, the now enhanced and fully searchable database of all the nationally designated heritage assets in England (list.english-heritage.org.uk) which we launched in May 2011.

A crucial tool for tracking the condition of the most important parts of the historic environment is, of course, the *Heritage at Risk Register*. By 2011, 50.3% of the entries which were on the 1999 baseline Register had been removed. The 2011 Register was published alongside the largest ever research project into the condition of England's industrial heritage. It revealed that listed industrial buildings are more at risk than almost any other category of heritage; almost 11% of Grade I and II* industrial buildings are at risk compared to 3% for Grade I and II* buildings at risk as a whole. In recognition of the particular challenges these buildings present, English Heritage has created a new section on its website that offers advice to developers on re-using industrial buildings.

For wider application and by way of a pragmatic response to the current economic climate, in October we published a new guide to keeping buildings safe from decay or in temporary use, *Vacant Historic Buildings: An Owner's Guide to Temporary Uses, Maintenance and Mothballing*. We also updated our guidance on how to save at risk buildings: *Stopping the Rot*.

October also saw the first English Heritage Angel Awards. This new initiative, founded by Andrew Lloyd Webber, is based on the *Heritage at Risk Register*. It celebrates the efforts of local people in rescuing their heritage. Six winners were chosen for their perseverance and imagination as well as the scale of the challenge and how well it had been tackled. Their awards recognised craftsmanship, the restoration of a cemetery, the best rescue of an industrial building or site and of a historic place of worship.

Rescuing and securing the future of heritage at risk was the motivation behind English Heritage adding the Grade I listed medieval barn at Harmondsworth, Middlesex, to the National Heritage Collection in October. While English Heritage has had to reprioritise in order to manage within its reduced budget, we can still respond in a true heritage emergency. Harmondsworth Barn is one of the most complete medieval barns in England; this intervention will halt the further deterioration of this exceptionally significant historic building and open it to the public.

English Heritage continues to be directly involved in the protection and management of the historic environment through its advice and grants. In 2011/12 English Heritage was consulted on 20,358 planning cases. We have been closely involved in the large-scale development proposed for the docks area of Liverpool that will cause damage to the Liverpool Maritime Mercantile City World Heritage Site. Another high profile and controversial project, the High Speed 2 rail link, has undergone various modifications to lessen its impact on nationally significant buildings and landscapes and English Heritage will continue to work with HS2 and their consultants to minimise the harm to the historic environment. We gave £31 million in grants this year. A grant of £250,000 to the Grade I listed St George's Theatre in Great Yarmouth will help towards the repair and conversion of the theatre, formerly the baroque Chapel of St George, into a more flexible arts venue. English Heritage is matching £1 million from the Andrew Lloyd Webber Foundation for the Heritage at Risk Challenge Fund administered by The Architectural Heritage Fund. In this, the first year of the fund, the Coker Rope and Sail Trust in Somerset, George Street Chapel in Oldham and Clophill Heritage Trust in Bedfordshire were awarded grants.

We are very pleased to be working with Government to take forward its proposal to improve the system of protection under the heading of the Penfold Review. The proposals fall into two parts, the first of which should be legislated for shortly. They are intended to make the system easier and quicker for owners while not reducing the levels of heritage protection.

Chief Executive's Report

The National Heritage Collection

We were delighted to welcome 5.2 million paying visitors last year. In addition around 6 million people took advantage of the many properties where admission is free. English Heritage membership rose from just over 1 million to 1.12 million. We estimate around 450,000 people enjoyed our events programme.

English Heritage carried out a review of its opening hours last year. This was in part a response to the CSR but more particularly a recognition that only 4% of total visits take place on winter weekdays and that opening arrangements were not consistent across the properties. As a result, last winter all staffed properties with the exception of Stonehenge, Old Sarum and Kenwood House, went down to weekend only opening. However the number of staffed properties open between November and March increased from 62 to 74 and almost 300 free sites remained open all year. These changes had the additional benefit of delivering a simpler and more consistent opening regime which is easier for visitors to understand. In conjunction with these changes, we greatly enhanced our winter events programme, quadrupling their number to 400, of which roughly half were for members and the rest available to all.

Online visitor numbers continue to grow with visits totalling nearly 10 million last year. This year we have begun work on digitising English Heritage Archives, formerly the National Monuments Record, following Heritage Lottery Fund funding of £1.76 million. This started with the oldest and most valuable photographs from the Aerofilms Collection, a unique air photographs archive with almost 19,000 negatives having gone through the preservation process so far. In spring 2011 we launched the first phase of Portico, an online library of resources for those interested in researching the history and significance of the National Heritage Collection.

Working closely with television companies has brought both more visitors and a wider audience to the National Heritage Collection. Both Audley End and J W Evans, the Birmingham silverware factory English Heritage rescued for the nation in 2009, featured in the primetime BBC1 series, *Britain's Hidden Heritage*, last summer. English Heritage was also closely involved with BBC2's *A History of Ancient Britain*, the first popular TV series to tackle the complete story of prehistoric Britain. The eight-part series featured many of our free sites and the BBC's Learning Campaign used our advice and educational materials. BBC2's *The Culture Show* produced a whole series of films about the inaugural English Heritage Angel Awards which were shown over six weeks and covered all the heritage rescue projects shortlisted for awards.

This year saw the establishment of the English Heritage Foundation which is an independent charity that exists to support and help raise money for English Heritage properties and collections. The Foundation has been working closely with English Heritage to support the Caring for Kenwood project, and in June made funds available for education resources at Wroxeter Roman City. We were very grateful to receive £987,000 this year from legacies and donations including sums received from the English Heritage Foundation.

These funds, alongside the income we generate from visitors and membership enable us to continue to invest to give our visitors the best possible day out. In June 2011 a major new exhibition opened at Dover Castle. It re-creates the Dunkirk evacuation through state-of-the-art effects in the same historic tunnels where the 'Operation Dynamo' rescue operation was masterminded. In August, the first phase of a 20-year restoration project at Wrest Park in Bedfordshire was completed, following the award of a £1.14 million Heritage Lottery Fund grant. Within the French-inspired mansion, the conservatory and Countess's Sitting Room have been restored and opened to the public while a new exhibition tells the story of the estate, its evolution and its personalities. New facilities also include a visitor centre, café and play area. As part of the project, eight historic gardens' apprentices are gaining valuable skills and qualifications.

Volunteers play an increasingly important role in supporting our work and this year we conducted our first national evaluation of volunteering at English Heritage. Of our 830 registered volunteers, 98% said they were happy with their volunteering role and 97% said they would recommend volunteering with English Heritage in the future.

Chief Executive's Report

At the end of March 2012 the long-needed refurbishment of the museum at Housesteads was completed. The building itself, a museum displaying artefacts from Hadrian's Wall for many decades, was in need of substantial repair. At the same time the opportunity was taken to completely redisplay the existing collection, as well as putting new pieces on display for the first time, and seeing the return of the statue of Victory to the site, on loan, after 150 years. A new CGI film offers an exciting new introduction to the Housesteads story for visitors of all ages and backgrounds. Along with the new introductory exhibition at Carlisle Castle, telling the story of the most besieged castle in England's history, these investments demonstrate the importance of the Hadrian's Wall corridor and our commitment to it.

The majority of our volunteers are involved in our Discovery Visits programme where they lead school children in exploring and learning from our sites. English Heritage was therefore delighted to be awarded funding from the Department for Education for the Heritage Schools Initiative. Working with the heritage sector, the £2.7 million over three years will be used to encourage the use of local heritage in delivering the curriculum.

This year English Heritage won the final permissions for the Stonehenge Environmental Improvements Programme. The project is now being delivered without any taxpayers' money. The £27 million project, spearheaded by English Heritage with the support of a wide range of partners including the National Trust and the Heritage Lottery Fund, will enable visitors to enjoy Stonehenge with world-class visitor facilities, reduced interference from traffic and with greater access to the wider landscape. In 2011/12 we have raised just under £2.5 million in additional private donations towards the improvements.

Improving our service and efficiency

Efficiency has been at the forefront of our minds this year. We have examined the services we provide in order to be more efficient in the future, with the aim of only doing the things which are essential to protect the historic environment and which others cannot do.

Investing in the National Heritage Collection such as the work at Wrest Park and Dover Castle is a key factor in our commercial success in recent years. These developments at well-visited sites have seen an increase in visitor numbers, with good commercial returns on our investments, while enhancing the experience of visiting the nation's collection of historic places. They enabled us to eliminate the operating deficit on opening the properties in our care which we did in 2009. We achieved a net surplus from opening our sites to the public this year of £5.2 million, an increase of £0.9 million since last year.

However we still face the problem of a significant maintenance deficit backlog of more than £54 million. We were able to increase expenditure on conservation by £2.27 million to £13.88 million this year but still believe that our expenditure in this area should be at least 6% per annum higher.

We have made significant procurement savings by negotiating new procurement contracts this year, making cost and time savings through standardisation of products and the use of a single point of order. Through our Voluntary Options Scheme we have sought to achieve permanent savings to our pay bill. We have offered staff alternative working patterns, partial retirement and Voluntary Exit, all constituting permanent pay bill savings. The other elements of the scheme, additional holiday purchase and unpaid leave, have generated more short term savings.

Dr Simon Thurley
Chief Executive

Progress Against Funding Agreement

Priority	Progress
Promote sustainable development	1. English Heritage was very pleased to be able to make a positive contribution to the wording of the National Planning Policy Framework (NPPF). We have prepared briefing on the NPPF, including an online training presentation and will hold free training events around the country over the coming months.
	2. We are in discussion with the Department for Communities and Local Government concerning their review of guidance to support the NPPF. Our existing guidance notes, such as that for enabling development, will be reviewed for concordance with the NPPF on a prioritised basis.
	3. English Heritage is working closely with DCMS on the 'Penfold' reforms aimed at improving the efficiency of non-planning consent procedures. English Heritage has also implemented a plan agreed with the Department for Business, Innovation and Skills to improve English Heritage's contribution to the planning system.
	4. The National Planning Department is undergoing a restructuring of its services in part to ensure it can best facilitate sustainable development, taking account of the Localism Act, changes in public service resources and the economic climate.
	5. We continue to provide efficient and cogent casework advice, engaging in pre-application advice wherever possible. In 2011/12: • 14.9% of our staff's advice time was spent on pre-application advice; • 297 heritage assets were removed from the Heritage at Risk Register for positive reasons (6.5%); and, • 94.7% of requests for English Heritage advice were processed within the agreed deadline.

Progress Against Funding Agreement

Priority	Progress
Focus activities in areas where English Heritage provides a distinctive service and reduce any areas of overlap with other bodies	1. While English Heritage has reduced its financial contribution to the Repair Grants for Places of Worship scheme we continue to administer and provide specialist advice on the scheme, on behalf of English Heritage and the Heritage Lottery Fund (HLF), and to fund those who object to receiving the proceeds of a lottery on moral grounds. The total amount of money available through this grant stream has not changed as the HLF has independently increased its contribution.
	2. The National Planning Department has examined the needs of the historic environment, the functions of other bodies that may satisfy those needs and the most efficient way in which English Heritage can continue to provide a distinctive and necessary service in light of the NPPF and the Localism Act. Restructuring to best facilitate that role will take place later in 2012.
	3. The National Heritage Protection Plan has now completed its first year of operation. It is a national framework for bringing together work by English Heritage and other partners within the sector to protect the historic environment. It will allow us to re-align and apply the full range of our expertise and resources most efficiently and effectively towards protection activities carried out directly by English Heritage or towards supporting others in their protection of what is valued and significant. It should lead to shared objectives, aligned activities and, where possible, pooling of resources to achieve more in combination than the sum of the separate parts. The activities set out within the Plan were consulted on widely and an advisory board has been set up to advise on the content and development of the Plan.
	4. English Heritage is running a project jointly with others called 'Historic Environment: Local Authority Capacity' (HELAC). It is a response to the cuts in resources in local authorities and its aims are to consider ways in which to retain a focus on strategic heritage outcomes, reduce unnecessary bureaucracy and process and pool resources across public bodies and engage civic societies more effectively. The key messages from the project include: management and protection of the historic environment requires properly qualified professionals regardless of model; stakeholders respect in-house services and their values; and there are opportunities and limits in involving others, such as the third sector, in the provision of historic environment activities.
	5. The co-ordination of Heritage Open Days has transferred from English Heritage to a consortium of the National Trust, Heritage Alliance and Civic Voice, with effect from 1 November. English Heritage will continue to provide grant aid for a further three years whilst the consortium develops its longer-term future strategy and funding.
	6. English Heritage is providing support to The Heritage Alliance to help the sector nurture philanthropic giving.

Priority	Progress
Continue designation and planning advice service, and implement actions agreed from designation strategy	1. The Designation Director is pursuing the tasks set out in the designation strategy, which looks at various ways of improving the efficiency and usefulness of designation (such as the listing of buildings and the scheduling of monuments). The details of how the improvements will be achieved are the subject of ongoing meetings between English Heritage and DCMS. 2. One aspect of the new approach to designation under the National Heritage Protection Plan is to focus more on 'strategic' designation. That is designation led by research into categories of heritage assets and areas that are most important and would most benefit from designation, as compared with reactive 'spot-listing' in response to public applications. This year 37.5% of designation was strategic. 3. Commentary on the English Heritage planning advice service and changes to it is given above.
Continue grants for heritage at risk and implement actions agreed from the Buildings at Risk strategy	1. Recent changes to grant funding are mentioned above. Otherwise English Heritage grant funding for heritage at risk remains in place. 2. English Heritage has agreed a plan of action with DCMS aimed at improving the prospects for long-term heritage at risk.
Continue the conservation and maintenance of sites in English Heritage's care	1. One of English Heritage's corporate targets is to improve the condition of the historic estate as evidenced by: a) a reduction in unplanned maintenance to 20% of the planned maintenance budget and b) a reduction in cyclical maintenance spend by 10% to redeploy to planned maintenance, by April 2015. This is currently on target. 2. The National Heritage Collection is increasingly self-sustaining, producing an operating surplus of £5.2 million, £0.9 million ahead of last year.
Increase self-generated income and philanthropic contributions	1. The English Heritage Foundation was established in February 2011 as an independent charitable trust (registered charity no. 1140351). The Foundation's objective is to fundraise for English Heritage properties. It has decided to focus its fundraising to support key projects within the English Heritage capital investment programme. 2. In 2011/12 English Heritage secured £7.9 million through fundraising. We received £21.5 million in charitable giving, including membership income and third party grants. English Heritage's percentage of charitable giving to Grant in Aid was 17.5%, a similar figure to last year. Earned income for 2011/12 was £52.1 million. This was £2.1 million ahead of target, largely due to a better than budget performance at sites. 3. The new Stonehenge visitor centre and the environmental improvements are a key element in the plan to increase self-generated income. All necessary permissions have now been secured and preparations for a start on site are well underway. We remain on target for completion of the visitor centre in October 2013 and all the remaining environmental improvement works by the end of 2014. 4. Investment in the National Heritage Collection is key to growing commercial income. The capital programme we have set for this Spending Review period is based on considerable levels of third party funding. Including Stonehenge, our capital programme for the four years totals £54.4 million, of which only £13.7 million is Grant in Aid funded. 5. At the end of 2011/12 English Heritage's volunteers had increased to 830.

Progress Against Funding Agreement

Priority	Progress
Continue to support the Cultural Olympiad	1. English Heritage supported the setting up of the 'Discovering Places' project, which is part of the Cultural Olympiad (discoveringplaces.co.uk/about-us). 2. English Heritage is hosting a number of events at its sites that will have a sports-related theme. The Olympic torch relay will visit some of our sites, such as Stonehenge. 3. English Heritage published *The British Olympics: British Olympic Heritage from 1612 to 2012,* the penultimate title in the eight-title *Played in Britain* series. They all describe Britain's sporting heritage using data and photographs from English Heritage's archives. We will publish *Played in London* in September. For more information see www.playedinbritain.co.uk/books.php. The summer 2012 edition of *Conservation Bulletin* has a theme of sporting heritage. 4. Work is underway on a project on disability history, the results of which are expected to be published in November. Building on interest generated by the Paralympics, the web-based project will tell the story of the history of disability and how it has been perceived through buildings.
Operate within programme and administration control totals	1. English Heritage's 2011/12 administration spend was well within control totals and overall resource spend was within an estimated 0.1% of control totals set out in our Funding Agreement letter.

English Heritage Key Performance Indicators

Aim 1 - Identify and Protect our Most Important Heritage		2011/12
CKPI 01	Number of new designations	495
CKPI 02	Percentage of designation outcomes that are reactive/strategic	63% reactive 37% strategic
CKPI 03	Number of new list descriptions for existing designated assets	991
CKPI 04	Number of requests for English Heritage advice processed	20,358
CKPI 05	Percentage of requests for English Heritage advice processed within the agreed deadline	94.7%
CKPI 06	Percentage spend on priority defects	29.3%
CKPI 07	Total number of heritage assets on the Heritage at Risk Register	5,657
CKPI 08	Value of grants given	£31.37m

Aim 2 - Champion England's Heritage		2011/12
CKPI 09	Stakeholder survey	Not yet available

Aim 3 - Support Owners, Local Authorities and Voluntary Organisations to look after England's Heritage		2011/12
CKPI 10	Number of users of English Heritage online resources	9.94m
CKPI 11	Number of people trained	1,136 (estimated)
CKPI 12	Number of unique visitors to the HELM website	442,004
CKPI 13	Number of pieces of advice and guidance published online	76 guidelines and standards documents

English Heritage Key Performance Indicators

Aim 4 - Help People Appreciate and Enjoy England's National Story		2011/12
CKPI 14	Number of paying visitors	5.22m
CKPI 15	Number of educational visits to historic properties, collections and tailored learning activities and resources	637,984
CKPI 16	Number of volunteers	830
CKPI 17	Number of members	1.12m
CKPI 18	Visitor experience (out of 10)	8.8
CKPI 19	Net surplus from opening the National Heritage Collection to the public	£5.20m

Aim 5 - Achieve Excellence, Openess and Efficiency in all we do		2011/12
CKPI 20	Amount raised through fundraising by English Heritage Development Department	£7.92m
CKPI 21	Earned income as a proportion of total income	29.7%
CKPI 22	Ratio of charitable giving to Grant in Aid	17.5%
CKPI 23	Amount of Grant in Aid to the National Heritage Collection	£20.84m

The Year in Numbers

Capacity Building

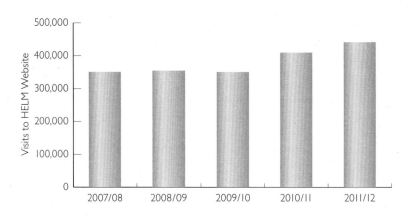

Paying Visitors

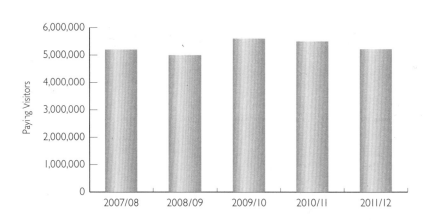

Members

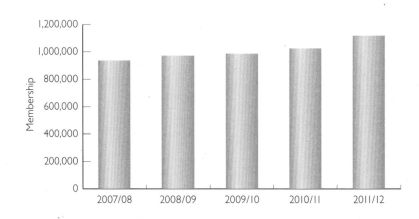

Net Surplus from Opening
the National Heritage
Collection to the Public

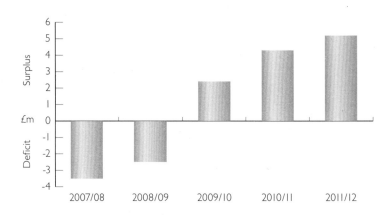

The Year in Numbers

Total Income and Grant in Aid (£m)

▨ Total non-GIA Income	54.2
▨ Grant in Aid	121.2
Total	**175.4**

Earned, Operating and Investment Income (£m)

■ Admisssion Income	15.4
▨ Retail and Catering Income	12.6
▨ Membership Income	19.7
■ Other Earned Income	4.4
▨ Donations, Grants and Other Operating Income	1.9
■ Interest	0.2
Total	**54.2**

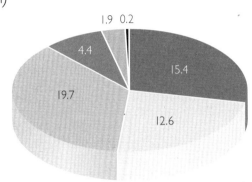

Grant Expenditure (£m)

■ Buildings and Monuments	11.2
▨ Conservation Areas	2.3
▨ Catherdrals and Other Places of Worship	7.2
■ Historic Environment	5.1
■ Other	5.6
Total	**31.4**

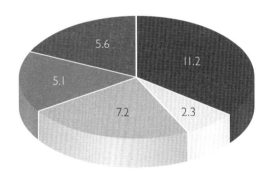

Total Expenditure (£m)

■ Grants	31.4
▨ Heritage Protection & Planning	32.7
▨ National Collections	73.0
■ Corporate & Support Services	26.8
■ Depreciation & Amortisation	6.2
Total	**170.1**

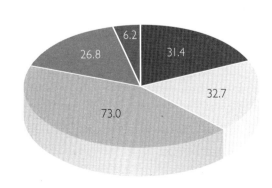

Sustainability Report

Greenhouse Gas Emissions

	2011/12	2010/11
Non-Financial Indicators (tCO₂e: tonnes of CO₂ equivalent)		
Total Gross Emissions for Scopes 1 & 2	10,629	11,109
Total Net Emissions for Scopes 1 & 2 (i.e. less reductions – e.g. green tariffs)	10,629	11,109
Gross emissions Scope 3 business travel	641	1,691
Other Scope 3 emissions measured	2	2
Related Energy Consumption (KWh: kilowatthour)		
Electricity: Non-Renewable	15,602,043	15,386,767
Electricity: Renewable	-	-
Gas	7,966,231	10,917,724
LPG	173,320	209,028
Other	2,927,507	3,102,075
Financial Indicators		
Expenditure on Energy	£1,925k	£1,756k
CRC License Expenditure (2010 onwards)	-	-
CRC Income from Recycling Payments	-	
Expenditure on accredited offsets (e.g. GCOF)	-	-
Expenditure on official business travel	£2,326k	£2,662k

Note: The scopes and conversion rates are set out in the 2011 Guidelines to Defra/DECC's Greenhouse Gas Protocol Conversion Factors for Company Reporting.

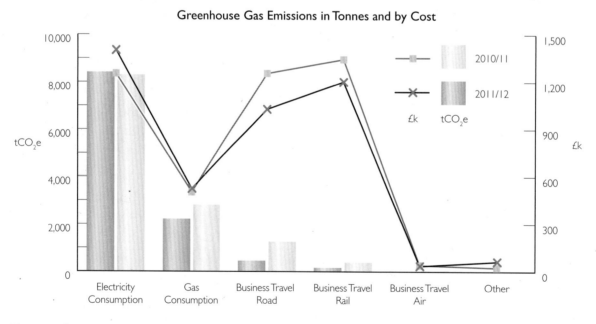

Greenhouse Gas Emissions in Tonnes and by Cost

The on-going programme of installing smart meters at the top 40 sites has proved a success in providing English Heritage with a mechanism to control energy usage. The results of this can be seen in the reduced level of emissions produced this year. This is vital to counter rising costs. The programme will continue to be expanded to include all types of energy consumption.

The drop in emissions from business travel can be linked to the winter closure of our sites. In addition, major restructuring has led to less travel but this may increase as working patterns return to normal. Both of these have helped to reduce the total spend when costs have risen.

ENGLISH HERITAGE ANNUAL REPORT AND ACCOUNTS 2011/12

Sustainability Report

Waste

Non-Financial Indicators (tonnes)		2011/12	2010/11
Total waste		480	540
Hazardous waste	Total	-	-
Non hazardous waste	Landfill	213	152
	Reused/Recycled	267	382
	Incinerated/energy from waste	-	6
Financial Indicators			
Total disposal cost		£45k	£43k
Hazardous waste - Total disposal cost		-	-
Non hazardous waste - Total disposal cost	Landfill	£21k	£31k
	Reused/Recycled	£24k	£12k
	Incinerated/energy from waste	-	-

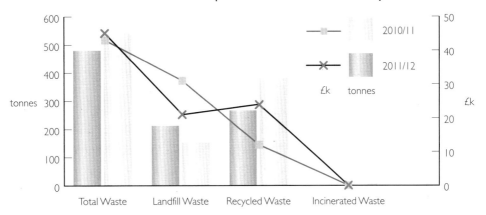

Waste Volumes and Disposable Routes in Tonnes and by Cost

Data for volumes of waste produced in 2010/11 were based on estimated figures. For this second year and ongoing, the organisation has been able to collect accurate information. This year's table also includes tonnes of waste from one major project for construction (Landfill: 21 tonnes, Recycling: 17 tonnes). Despite this, there has been a reduction on the amount produced. Next year will see a larger number of major construction projects being included as part of the Construction Industry Regulations where a Site Waste Management Plan is required.

Water

Non-Financial Indicators (m³)	Water Consumption	Supplied	128,136	124,854
		Abstracted	-	-
Financial Indicators	Water Supply Costs		£226k	£232k

The header row for the Water table reads: | | | | 2011/12 | 2010/11 |

Water usage and costs appears to have remained relatively constant year on year. English Heritage has now extended the smart metering programme to include water resources. This should provide improved management information on water usage in the future.

Management Commentary

Introduction

The Historic Buildings and Monuments Commission for England is a body corporate established on 1 April 1984 by the National Heritage Act 1983. It has up to 17 Commissioners appointed by the Secretary of State for Culture, Media and Sport (DCMS) and is an Executive Non-Departmental Public Body sponsored by DCMS. 'English Heritage' is its informal name. English Heritage is the Government's statutory adviser on the historic environment and our role is to help people understand, value, care for and enjoy England's rich historic environment. Our aims are set out in our Corporate Plan for 2011-15 which was published in May 2011.

Our strategic direction is overseen by a Board of Commissioners that delegates operational management to a Chief Executive appointed by them. The Chief Executive also serves as Accounting Officer on behalf of DCMS. The Chief Executive is supported by an Executive Board comprising the Executive Directors of English Heritage's four operational groups: Heritage Protection and Planning, National Advice and Information, National Collections, and Resources.

English Heritage's Funding Agreement, signed with DCMS, the Department for Communities and Local Government and the Department for Environment, Food and Rural Affairs, with our Management Statement and Financial Memorandum and our Corporate Plan, provide the context and framework for our work. A review of progress against our Funding Agreement starts on page six of this report. We also work with other Government departments and a range of agencies such as Natural England on issues relating to heritage.

Our relationship with the local authorities across England is central to our work. We provide advice and guidance as part of our role as a statutory consultee in the planning system, and on local and strategic plans, policy statements and other public initiatives. We also support them by providing training and advice for members and officers, mainly through the Historic Environment-Local Management (helm.org.uk) portal which is used by local authority decision-makers all over England.

The heritage sector comprises a few large organisations and several hundred smaller voluntary organisations, local groups and commercial operators, many of which are members of The Heritage Alliance. English Heritage now supports The Alliance to provide the secretariat for the Historic Environment Forum which exists to strengthen advocacy work and communications and to co-ordinate initiatives such as the annual audit of the historic environment, *Heritage Counts*.

Trends and factors underlying English Heritage's performance during 2011/12

The 2010 Spending Review resulted in a 32% real terms cut in funding for English Heritage over the period 2011-2015. Implementation of the plan to manage within the reduced level of funding was the overriding issue which had an impact on performance during the year.

The plan encompassed four main areas covering restructuring, and, as a consequence, some cuts in services, reductions in our grants programme, delivery of further efficiencies and continued commercial growth.

The reduction in staffing levels was a very regrettable but inevitable consequence of the scale of reduction in our Grant in Aid funding. The reductions implemented in-year relate primarily to a revised Group structure, implementation of reduced winter opening hours in the National Heritage Collection and changes in the management structure of our Historic Properties department.

Visitor attendance at our properties grew again in line with the year-on-year growth of the previous two years, with numbers of paying visitors for 2011/12 at just over 5.2 million. This increase reflects the continuing effects of a strong domestic market, the growth of group business from overseas and our continued investment in the Collection.

Management Commentary

Trends and factors likely to affect English Heritage's future performance

During 2012/13 we will be implementing the final major structural change required as a result of reduced Government funding. This relates to the National Planning department and follows a review of advice and grants with the aim of improving our contribution to sustainable development in England. We will also implement further reductions in our grants programme. Apart from these measures, the organisation should enter a period of welcome stability as the effect of the changes implemented over the last 12 months bed in. 2012/13 will be the second year of implementation, within English Heritage, of the public sector wide pay freeze. The impact of this on staff morale and our ability to recruit and retain staff is a cause of concern and will be monitored closely.

A key issue for English Heritage is the scale of the priority defects that need to be addressed on our historic estate. This has arisen because declining funding has meant it has not been possible to allocate sufficient funds to our maintenance programmes. Our Asset Management Plan provides comprehensive condition surveys of all our properties. This shows that the investment required to bring the estate up to the required benchmark condition is estimated to be £54 million. Of this, £6 million of expenditure is deemed to be urgent.

For budgeting purposes, we have made no assumptions about the impact of the Olympics and the Diamond Jubilee on attendances and spending patterns, as views on this within the attractions market vary. We are optimistic about future years however, as it is hoped that the international exposure which Britain will gain from these events will result in an increase in overseas business.

Chief Executive's Statement

As Chief Executive I have a duty to report on English Heritage's policies and progress in certain matters which are set out here.

Disability equality
English Heritage's Disability Equality Scheme aims to increase participation by people with disabilities. The fifth annual progress report on the scheme was published on our website in summer 2011. In March 2012 self-reporting by the staff who responded identified that 2.1% have a disability and 97.9% declared that they do not. 7.2% did not provide the information. However our anonymous staff survey carried out in early 2010 indicated that 8% of our employees considered themselves to have a disability or long term health condition.

Gender equality
The English Heritage Gender Group monitors progress against an action plan each year and an updated report and revised action plan will be published on our website in summer 2012. In March 2012 the gender profile of English Heritage staff was 59.6% female and 40.4% male.

Race equality
English Heritage's Race Equality Strategy was reviewed in 2010 and the revised strategy will form part of the English Heritage Single Equality Scheme when this is published later this year. In March 2012 self-reporting by staff identified that 97.9% of those who responded are from White ethnic groups and 2.1% are from non-White groups. 5.8% did not provide the information.

Sickness absence
The Average Working Days Lost (AWDL) per person for English Heritage is 4.8 for the financial year 2011/12 compared with 5.1 for 2010/11.

Sustainability
English Heritage's progress against its sustainability indicators can be found on page 14 of this report.

Safety management
In 2011/12 there were 482 reported accidents of which 42 were reportable to the Health and Safety Executive under statutory reporting regulations, compared with a total of 512 with 37 which were reportable in the previous year.

Management Commentary

Biodiversity, National Parks and Areas of Outstanding Natural Beauty (AONB)
English Heritage has duties to promote National Park and AONB purposes and biodiversity. During 2011/12 we engaged in the protected landscapes monitoring strategy project with Natural England and began work on refreshing the National Parks Joint Statement and AONB Accord.

Information and data security
English Heritage's progress in this area is reported within the Governance Statement which starts on page 25 of this report.

Open Government and Freedom of Information

English Heritage recognises the important role that access to information legislation (primarily the Freedom of Information Act 2000 and Environmental Information Regulations 2004) play in serving the public interest by promoting open discussion of public affairs and enhancing accountability. English Heritage makes a large volume of information available via its website (english-heritage.org.uk) including agendas and the public minutes and papers of the Commission and advisory committees and panels. In line with best practice we also have an online Information Disclosure Log which contains summaries of all of the information requests we receive and a selection of the responses that we have provided to them. In 2011/12 we processed 406 requests for information under access to information legislation, the majority of which concerned listing and scheduling, and planning related matters.

Dr Simon Thurley
Chief Executive

Directors' Report

Background Information

"English Heritage" is the name of the consolidation of the Historic Buildings and Monuments Commission for England (HBMCE), English Heritage Trading Limited and the Iveagh Bequest. Further details of English Heritage's organisational structure and background are included in the Management Commentary in the Annual Report.

Commissioners and Executive Board Members

The persons who served as Commissioners between 1 April 2011 and 27 June 2012 are detailed in note 12. Details of Executive Board members are given in the Remuneration Report.

Responsibilities of Commissioners

The key responsibilities of Commissioners are to ensure that the statutory responsibilities of English Heritage are undertaken; to provide expert advice and guidance on heritage matters; to establish the overall strategic direction of English Heritage; to oversee and monitor the planned performance against strategic objectives and targets; to ensure the highest standards of probity are used in the administration of funds and to maximise the economical, efficient and effective use of resources for the public good; to ensure the highest standards of corporate governance and to ensure the Commission acts within all statutory and regulatory requirements; to ensure, through the Chief Executive, that the Commission, as employer, acts in accordance with all relevant legislation and best practice; and to ensure that English Heritage conducts its dealings with the community in an open, responsive and accountable manner.

Register of Interests

English Heritage maintains a record of declarations of interest made by Commissioners. A copy of the Register of Interests is available from the Commission Secretariat Manager, English Heritage, 1 Waterhouse Square, 138-142 Holborn, London, EC1N 2ST.

Result for the Year

The net expenditure for the year ended 31 March 2012, after the transfer from the Development and Restricted Funds of £775,000 (2011: £112,000 transfer to the Development and Restricted Funds) and revenue to capital transfer of £1,083,000 (2011: nil) was £118,727,000 (2011: £134,397,000). The reduction in total expenditure resulted from the implementation of a restructuring programme with a resultant £8,611,000 reduction in payroll costs (note 15b), various other efficiency savings and the reduction of the grants programme by £3,430,000 from financial year 2010/11 (note 5). The operating surplus achieved as a result of operating sites opening to the public and related activities, was £5,200,000 (2011: £4,300,000).

Change to Accounting Policy

In accordance with the revised IAS 20 'Accounting for Government Grants', all capital grants other than Grant in Aid have been treated as revenue in the Statement of Comprehensive Net Expenditure, unless there is a condition of grant which has not been fulfilled (in which case the income should be deferred). Additional income recognised in 2011/12 totalled £2,855,000 (note 3). In addition, the EU Government Grant Reserve and Donated Asset Reserve have been reclassified within the Statement of Changes in Tax Payers Equity under IAS 8 'Accounting Policies, Changes in Accounting Estimates and Errors', with a resultant net movement of £1,299,000 as at 1 April 2010.

Post Balance Sheet Events

Post balance sheet events are disclosed in note 39. The Annual Report and Accounts were authorised for issue by the Accounting Officer on the date the Comptroller and Auditor General certified the accounts.

Directors' Report

Charitable Donations

English Heritage did not make any charitable donations exceeding £500 (2011: nil) during the financial year ended 31 March 2012.

Communications with Employees

English Heritage recognises the importance of effective communications in order to keep all employees informed, motivated and engaged. The communication channels include regular management briefings on key initiatives, weekly staff updates, the corporate intranet site and presentations made to staff by the Chief Executive which are also filmed and published on the intranet. English Heritage works with three recognised Trade Unions to develop appropriate employment policies, procedures and terms and conditions for all employees. Twice a year, Executive Board meets with representatives from the recognised Trade Unions at the full Whitley Council meeting which is chaired by the Chief Executive.

Confederation of British Industry Better Payment Practice Code

English Heritage is a member of the Confederation of British Industry scheme and has established a payment policy which complies with the principles of the Confederation of British Industry Better Payment Practice Code. The code requires that invoices should be paid by their due date or within 30 days of receipt, whichever is later. Invoices received but not paid at 31 March 2012 equated to 14 creditor days (2011: 12 days).

Audit Arrangements

The Comptroller and Auditor General has been auditor of HBMCE since 1 April 2004 and English Heritage Trading Limited from 1 April 2008. Saffery Champness have been independent examiners of the Iveagh Bequest since 1997.

Disclosure of Relevant Audit Information

As Accounting Officer, I have taken all the steps that ought to have been taken to make myself aware of any relevant audit information and to establish that the National Audit Office is aware of that information. So far as I am aware, there is no relevant audit information of which the National Audit Office is unaware.

Dr Simon Thurley
Chief Executive
27 June 2012

Remuneration Report

Remuneration and Human Resources Committee

The objective of the Remuneration and Human Resources Committee is to review and advise on English Heritage's Human Resources strategy to ensure that it is contributing effectively to the success of the organisation.

It is also the objective of the Committee to review the reward and remuneration of English Heritage's staff so as to:

• demonstrate that reward and remuneration is considered by a Committee which has no personal interest in the outcome of its advice and which gives due regard to the interests of the public and the financial health of the organisation; and

• ensure that staff are fairly rewarded for their individual contributions to the organisation's overall performance within DCMS and HM Treasury delegated limits.

In carrying out the above, the Committee provides advice and oversight external to English Heritage management, necessary to demonstrate public accountability.

The Committee is scheduled to meet at least three times each year, although in 2011/12 it met four times. It comprises no fewer than five members, who are appointed by the Chair of Commission. At least three members must be Commissioners, and one of these positions is taken by the Chair of Commission. One of the other Commissioners chairs the Committee. Mrs Joyce Bridges CBE was Acting Chair for the first Committee meeting in 2011/12 and the Chair of the Committee for the remainder of 2011/12 was Professor Ronald Hutton.

Executive Board Remuneration Policy

The remuneration of Executive Board is determined by the Remuneration and Human Resources Committee. Pay ranges have been established for each post by reference to the relevant external market data, and changes to base pay are reviewed annually by the Committee in that context.

Executive Board Service Contracts

Executive Board members are employed on continuous contracts and are required to give three months' notice of termination of employment by resignation. The Chief Executive is also on a continuous contract and is required to give six months' notice of termination of employment by resignation. Early terminations of contract by English Heritage are dealt with in accordance with the rules of the Civil Service Compensation Scheme.

The only Executive Board members with a contractual performance bonus arrangement are the Chief Executive and the Director of Resources.

The bonuses are payable for the achievement of specific performance targets and objectives and are a maximum of 20 per cent of basic salary for the Chief Executive and 8 per cent of basic salary for the Director of Resources.

Following the end of each financial year the Remuneration and Human Resources Committee assesses the Chief Executive's and the Director of Resource's performance against their annual targets and objectives and determines the rate of their performance related bonus.

Remuneration Report

Emoluments of Executive Board

	Emoluments 2012 £'000	2011 £'000	Total accrued pension at age 60[1] 2012 £'000	Total lump sum at age 60[1] 2011 £'000	Real annual increase in pension £'000	Real annual increase in lump sum £'000	CETV[2] 2012 £'000	2011 £'000	Real annual increase in CETV £'000
Simon Thurley Chief Executive	**163**	150	**39**	116	**1**	**4**	**651**	579	23
Keith Harrison Director of Resources	**132**	120	**12**	-	**2**	-	**112**	84	18
Edward Impey Director of Heritage Protection and Planning	**112**	112	**18**	-	**1**	-	**252**	219	11
Deborah Lamb Director of National Advice and Information	**101**	101	**40**	-	**1**	-	**581**	521	10
Mark Pemberton[3] Director of National Collections	**128**	124	**58**	173	**1**	**2**	**1,298**	1,187	11

Notes

1   Balances as at 31 March 2012.

2   The actuarial factors used to calculate CETVs were changed in 2011/12. The CETVs at 31 March 2011 and 31 March 2012 have both been calculated using the new factors, for consistency. The CETV at 31 March 2011 therefore differs from the corresponding figure in last year's report which was calculated using the previous factors.

3   Emoluments for 2011/12 include back pay of £1,000 relating to 2010/11.

Reporting bodies are required to disclose the relationship between the remuneration of the highest paid director in their organisation and the median remuneration of the organisation's workforce. The remuneration of the highest paid director in English Heritage in the financial year 2011/12 was £163,000. This was 8.25 times the median remuneration of the workforce, which was £19,755. The median salary within English Heritage is relatively low due to a large number of part-time staff. Salaries also reflect a regional pay structure. In 2011/12, nil (2010/11: nil) employees received remuneration in excess of the highest paid director. Total remuneration includes salary, non-consolidated performance-related pay, benefits-in-kind as well as severance payments. It does not include employer pension contributions and the cash equivalent transfer value of pensions.

Performance Related Awards

Emoluments include gross salary and awards. No benefits in kind were paid during the year (2011: nil). The Chief Executive was the highest paid employee. His total emoluments for the year of £163,000 (2011: £150,000) comprise basic salary of £136,000 (2011: £136,000) and a performance related award of £27,000 (2011: £14,000). The Director of Resources' emoluments for the year of £132,000 (2011: £120,000) comprise basic salary of £120,000 (2011: £120,000) and a performance related award of £12,000 (2011: nil). Exceptionally, the Committee made an award of 10% in 2011/12. The Director of Resources was awarded a performance related award of £10,000 in 2011 but declined to take it. The remaining Directors were not eligible for a bonus.

Pension Benefits

Pension benefits to English Heritage staff are provided through the Principal Civil Service Pension Scheme (PCSPS). The value of the annual pension and lump sum at 60 and the real increases thereon and the cash equivalent transfer values (CETV) shown above include accumulated pension benefits from English Heritage service, plus benefits resulting from any additional contributions and any sums transferred in from other pension schemes in respect of previous employment. The real annual increase in CETV excludes the cash value of accumulated pension benefits transferred from previous employment but includes the benefits resulting from such transfers. The total annual pension is calculated as either one-sixtieth or one-eightieth of pensionable pay for every year of service, depending on the pension option chosen by the employee. Employer's contributions into the PCSPS in respect of the above employees totalled £145,000 (2011: £160,000). Employers contributions in 2010/11 included £19,000 in respect of Mr Stephen Bee who left under Compulsory Early Retirement during the year. Further details of the PCSPS scheme are included in note 16.

Remuneration Report

The emoluments section of the Remuneration Report is audited. The Commissioners of English Heritage are not viewed to be "Directors" as defined by the Government Financial Reporting Manual. Details of the Commissioners and their emoluments are included in note 12.

Simon Thurley

Dr Simon Thurley
Chief Executive
27 June 2012

Statement of Commissioners' and Chief Executive's Responsibilities

Under paragraph 12(2) of Schedule 3 of the National Heritage Act 1983, the Commissioners are required to prepare a statement of accounts for each financial year in the form and on the basis determined by the Secretary of State with the consent of HM Treasury. The accounts are prepared on an accruals basis and must show a true and fair view of English Heritage's state of affairs at the year end and of its income and expenditure and cash flows for the financial year.

In preparing the accounts the Commissioners are required to:

- observe the Accounts Direction issued by the Secretary of State, including the relevant accounting and disclosure requirements, and apply suitable accounting policies on a consistent basis;

- make judgements and estimates on a reasonable basis;

- state whether applicable accounting standards have been followed, and disclose and explain any material departures from these in the financial statements; and

- prepare the financial statements on the going concern basis, unless it is inappropriate to presume that the Commission will continue in operation.

The Accounting Officer for the Department for Culture, Media and Sport designated the Chief Executive of the Historic Buildings and Monuments Commission for England as the Accounting Officer for English Heritage. His relevant responsibilities as Accounting Officer, including his responsibility for the propriety and regularity of the public finances for which he is answerable and for the keeping of proper records, are set out by HM Treasury and published in *Managing Public Money*.

A copy of the Accounts Direction is available from English Heritage, 1 Waterhouse Square, 138-142 Holborn, London, EC1N 2ST.

Dr Simon Thurley
Chief Executive
27 June 2012

Baroness Andrews OBE
Chair
27 June 2012

Governance Statement

Scope of Responsibilities

English Heritage is a part-publicly funded body with statutory purposes set out principally in the National Heritage Act 1983. It is classified by Government as a non-departmental public body. English Heritage has set out its corporate aims in a published plan for the period 2011/2015. It has a Funding Agreement with Government that sets out a framework for the organisation's activities. It is governed by its Commission with a view to achieving its corporate and Funding Agreement aims within its statutory purposes in a manner that is impartial, objective, efficient, open and accountable.

In particular, the governance arrangements seek to achieve legal and regulatory compliance, the highest standards of probity and ethics (including compliance with the 'Nolan principles'), proportionate risk management, compliance with Government policy and guidance on managing public money, information asset management and governance generally.

As Accounting Officer, I have responsibility for maintaining a sound system of governance whilst managing risks and safeguarding the public funds and departmental assets for which I am personally responsible in accordance with the responsibilities assigned to me in *Managing Public Money*.

Governance Framework

Governance within English Heritage is exercised through:

- the Commission, the governing body comprising non-executive Commissioners as explained in the Directors' Report;

- an Executive Board, comprising four group directors and me, as the Accounting Officer. Each group director is personally accountable to me for the achievement of the aims and objectives of the organisation and the management of risks where they are wholly or partly the responsibility of their group. There are delegated authorities from the Chief Executive to group directors, and within each group, to make decisions and incur costs as specified in the Financial Memorandum and the Finance Manual; and

- the Audit Committee, which is an advisory committee of Commission with no executive authority. During this year the Committee has had an independent chair who was not a Commissioner followed by the incumbent who is a Commissioner. Generally there are three other members, at least one of whom is a Commissioner, but as there is presently a vacancy for one of the other roles, the Committee had just three members this year. All are appointed to the Committee by the Chair of Commission. The Committee's terms of reference include responsibility for advising on and monitoring the adequacy of risk management in English Heritage and the Committee receives half-yearly reports on corporate performance, including the management of risk and oversight of governance arrangements generally. The Committee carries out its work by testing and challenging the assurances I receive on the effectiveness of internal controls and risk management, the way in which these assurances are developed, and the management priorities on which they are based. The Committee may also seek contributions from others when it considers that its work can be enhanced by other specialist support. The Committee is also given the opportunity to comment on and challenge the assurances made in this statement. The Committee meets three times a year. This is less than the recommended four times (as suggested by the Corporate Governance Code 2011), but practice over a number of years has shown this to be sufficient in English Heritage given the cycle of reporting and business in the organisation.

Governance Statement

The membership of these boards is set out below with the attendance record for this year. Members have a broad range of experience in finance, risk management and governance generally. Details of individual experience can be found on the English Heritage website.

Commission	Meetings attended	Executive Board	Meetings attended	Audit Committee	Meetings attended
Baroness Andrews (Chair)	6/6	Dr Simon Thurley	17/17	Lynda Addison	2/2
Lynda Addison	6/6	Keith Harrison	16/17	Andrew Fane	2/2
Professor Sir Barry Cunliffe	5/6	Dr Edward Impey	16/17	Andy Karski	2/3
Peter Draper	4/5	Deborah Lamb	16/17	Martin Moore	1/1
David Fursdon	6/6	Mark Pemberton	16/17	John Walker	3/3
Professor Ronald Hutton	6/6				
Jane Kennedy	6/6				
Vice-Admiral Sir Tim Laurence	5/5				
Martin Moore	3/5				
Graham Morrison	5/5				
John Walker	6/6				
Baroness Young	4/5				

There are other advisory committees that advise staff and report to Commission: English Heritage Advisory Committee, London Advisory Committee, Designation Review Committee, Business Committee, Finance Committee and Remuneration/Human Resources Committee. Each has a distinct area of business and all except the Finance Committee have a mix of Commissioners and external expert advisers in their membership. There are also a number of advisory panels formed also of external experts who advise staff on technical fields.

Declarations of potential conflicts of interest are sought from all Commissioners and members of Executive Board, the English Heritage Advisory Committee and the London Advisory Committee every half-year and a register maintained. Declarations are also sought at each meeting in relation to the business on the agenda of all the above boards and committees. Where there is a material conflict the individual takes no part in the proceedings.

Accountability to Ministers is managed through the usual control mechanisms for Arm's Length Bodies. English Heritage has a Funding Agreement with DCMS and complies with a Management Statement and Financial Memorandum. English Heritage makes six-monthly progress reports to its Funding Agreement Monitoring Group which comprises representatives from DCMS, the departments for Communities and Local Government and for the Environment, Food and Rural Affairs and the Treasury. In addition I, as Accounting Officer, and the members of my Executive Board, have regular meetings with senior DCMS staff to discuss high level issues. Meetings with the Permanent Secretary and Ministers take place on specific issues as required.

Governance Statement

The Purpose of the System of Governance

The overriding purpose of our governance system is to maximise the potential of the organisation and its resources to achieve its aims and objectives.

Risk management is designed to manage performance and control risk to a reasonable level rather than to eliminate all risk of failure to achieve our aims. It can therefore only provide reasonable, and not absolute, assurance of effectiveness. Our approach is to identify and prioritise the risks to the achievement of our aims, to evaluate the likelihood of those risks being realised and the impact should they be realised, and to manage them effectively and economically.

The Method of Governance

The system of governance has continued in place in English Heritage for the financial year ended 31 March 2012 and up to the date of approval of the Annual Report and Accounts. It accords with Treasury guidance, including the Corporate Governance Code of Good Practice 2011 in so far as it is applicable to Arm's Length Bodies, save as mentioned above in relation to Audit Committee meeting frequency.

Commission has set aims for the organisation which were published in the Corporate Plan for 2011 to 2015. Executive Board has agreed corporate targets under each of the aims and has a number of key performance indicators that it uses to measure performance against the aims and targets. The Board also maintains a corporate risk register that helps the organisation to focus its resources on the most significant risks that it is facing.

An assessment of performance against aims, targets and risks is carried out by Executive Board and Audit Committee at half-year and year-end meetings. Audit Committee is robust in its scrutiny of performance and risk management and, when appropriate, will ask for further information on key targets and high risk issues. Commission reviews the year-end performance and risk reporting.

Responsibility for achieving corporate aims and targets and managing risks lies with Executive Board. The constituent group directors agree department targets and risks with each of the department directors that report to them that will achieve the corporate objectives. Department directors then delegate responsibility for delivering those department targets and controlling the risks to their staff as appropriate. Reports against those department targets and risks on a half-year cycle provide the information for Executive Board's review of overall corporate performance against the Corporate Plan and risk register.

Annual Letters of Assurance from group directors to me as Accounting Officer provide an additional level of comfort that risk is being properly managed throughout the organisation.

Responsibility for performance and risk management policy and coordination lies with the Governance and Legal Director who provides advice to Executive Board, particularly on the integrity of the corporate and departmental targets and risks when viewed in light of the Corporate Plan.

Our governance staff keep up-to-date with best practice in governance and risk management by attending appropriate courses from time to time and researching governance structures and risk management in comparable institutions.

Governance Statement

English Heritage maintains a risk management policy based on a risk appetite for taking only carefully calculated risks, where the potential benefits are judged to outweigh any negative impact that may occur if the risks were to materialise. Risk has been defined as 'the threat or possibility that an action or event will adversely or beneficially affect the organisation's ability to achieve its objectives'. The policy defines our risk management objectives, which are to:

- manage risk in accordance with best practice and encourage a culture of risk management across English Heritage;

- anticipate and meet changing social, environmental and legislative requirements that enable us to champion England's historic environment; and

- safeguard our assets and minimise opportunities for injury and damage and promote awareness of the need for risk management.

Monitoring the Effectiveness of Governance

As Accounting Officer, I have responsibility for reviewing the effectiveness of the system of governance. My review of the effectiveness is informed by: the work of the internal auditors; the advice of staff who have responsibility for the development and maintenance of the performance and risk management system; comments made by the external auditors in their management letter and other reports; the assurances gained from an annual programme of internal audit reviews and advice which is agreed by me, Executive Board and the Audit Committee; the assurances provided to me by each Executive Board member in their regular reports to me and the Executive Board generally; the performance reporting that stems from departmental performance reports that capture performance against targets and in controlling risks; and assurances gained from the work of specific committees, including Finance Committee and the Safety Council.

The results from my ongoing review of effectiveness are discussed with Executive Board and the Audit Committee. The Audit Committee provides assurances based on these reports to Commission.

Performance management including risk control is an ongoing process and will continue to be integral to strategic and operational planning, and to the delivery of the objectives and targets set out in our Funding Agreement and Corporate Plan. Performance management procedures and practice will also continue to be reviewed and developed in order to ensure effective control, good management and accountability.

Corporate Governance this Year

At the year-end Executive Board undertook a review of its effectiveness looking at all relevant matters including:

- the Board's own processes and practices;

- the views of Audit Committee, internal audit and other means of assurance;

- the formal performance and risk reporting from line management and the knowledge of directors from day-to-day management;

- the quality of data provided to the Board;

- the business of Commission and its committees;

- any other body's views or survey data that expressed a view on the performance of English Heritage.

The Board concluded that its operations had been satisfactory. As far as the process of governance was concerned, the data provided to the Board had been adequate for sound decision-making and risk management.

The following are highlights from the Board's review of its own reports and activities and those of Commission and its committees.

Governance Statement

The new means of corporate reporting and the Board's greater focus on strategic matters both presented a risk to the Board's control. The Board was satisfied that this was not happening in any significant way, but was concerned to test this again in future years.

This year was the first of four years of cuts in our Grant in Aid from Government. Our Grant in Aid this year was £8.7 million less than last year. Our Grant in Aid for the year 2014/2015 will be £32.9 million less than last year.

These changes have presented the greatest challenge to the organisation's good governance. With cuts of this scale, substantial restructuring of departments and loss of staff was sadly inevitable. A key risk for the Board was the consequent loss of expertise and a break in the continuity of management. Restructuring also threatened to draw management effort away from achieving the core aims and controlling the key risks. The majority of the restructuring of the organisation was completed this year, although one department (National Planning) will go through its reorganisation in 2012/2013.

As a consequence a lot of the focus of management activity and the internal audit monitoring programme has been put on the effect of staff changes. We have sought to ensure that systems of control and strategies to deliver on targets continue to be operated in a compliant and effective manner. The Board is satisfied that restructuring has been managed well so far and that the impact of the cuts on the organisation and its work has been minimised.

Partly to meet this challenge Executive Board and Audit Committee reviewed its performance and risk reporting systems and chose to significantly simplify the existing parallel arrangements. The new process is set out above. At Board and departmental level it brings risk and performance management and reporting together into one report. It provides a clear and simple means of communicating and monitoring the organisation's priorities for success. As such, it should prove an excellent means of ensuring that managers in their new roles post-restructuring are in no doubt as to the relevance of their work to the achievement of corporate targets and aims and in managing the corporate risks. As part of this review process, the Board refined its targets and identified new corporate risks. For example, targets such as those for tackling heritage at risk and for developing the National Heritage Collection have been made more specific; corporate risks have been created for a reduction in the level of protection for the historic environment, and for the level of change within the organisation having unforeseen consequences.

The National Heritage Protection Plan was implemented this year and was also a key means of controlling the risk of a loss of control through the changes in structure. The Plan sets the priorities for a large part of English Heritage's work. It optimises use of our resources by prioritising by risk and effectiveness the projects that English Heritage will take forward to achieve the protection of the historic environment. It is subject to external oversight by an expert committee of interested parties and reports publicly on progress. This transparency provides a healthy opportunity to others to challenge the usefulness and efficacy of work. It enables others to understand and build on our activities.

Achievement of our aims is to a significant degree reliant on existing heritage protection law and policy. There have been significant changes in law and policy this year, including the Localism Act and the National Planning Policy Framework. These key risks have been monitored very closely by Commission and Executive Board and their control has personally engaged a number of individuals from both.

Our corporate targets assume a level of income generation growth. A key element of that growth depends on the opening of a new visitor centre for Stonehenge. This year we have secured all the necessary permissions and so the risk of not delivering the new centre has lessened considerably. It remains our biggest single financial commitment, though, and a key priority for Commission and Executive Board.

Governance Statement

The world economic situation at present is of course a major concern for all. The Board is very mindful of the need to build resilience into its financial and work programming in order to be able to react to any significant changes in future income.

English Heritage has continued to make progress towards compliance with the mandatory requirements of the Security Policy Framework, developing an Information Asset Register, collecting information for the identified assets, training staff and raising awareness. New policies and guidelines are in development to be implemented over the next few months to further enhance information and data security in the organisation; these include a Clear Desk Policy, a Communications Policy and a Forensic Readiness Policy, which facilitates recovery from information security incidents. By summer 2012 English Heritage will be fully compliant with all aspects of the Payment Card Industry Data Security Standard (PCI DSS), an information security standard that increases controls around cardholder data to reduce credit card fraud. English Heritage has suffered no significant losses of protectively marked data during 2011/12, nor has it in prior years, and has made no report on the loss of personal protected information to the Information Commissioner's office.

Conclusion

There have been considerable challenges for the staff and senior management of English Heritage this year. The governance regime provides me with adequate assurance that the organisation continues to optimise its use of resources in achieving its objectives, whilst controlling risks to an appropriate degree. I believe the governance regime is fit for its purpose. My fellow Executive Board members and the Commission support this view.

Dr Simon Thurley
Chief Executive
27 June 2012

The Certificate and Report of the Comptroller and Auditor General to the Houses of Parliament

I have audited the financial statements comprising the Historic Buildings and Monuments Commission for England (HBMCE), English Heritage Trading Limited and the Iveagh Bequest (known collectively as 'English Heritage') for the year-ended 31 March 2012 under the National Heritage Act 1983. These comprise: the Consolidated Statement of Comprehensive Net Expenditure; the Consolidated Statement of Financial Position; the HBMCE Statement of Financial Position; the Consolidated Statement of Cash Flows; the HBMCE Statement of Cash Flows; the Consolidated Statement of Changes in Taxpayers' Equity; the HBMCE Statement of Changes in Taxpayers' Equity and the related notes. These financial statements have been prepared under the accounting policies set out within them. I have also audited the information in the Remuneration Report that is described in that report as having been audited.

Respective Responsibilities of the Commissioners, Chief Executive and Auditor

As explained more fully in the Statement of Commissioners' and Chief Executive's Responsibilities, the Commissioners and Chief Executive as Accounting Officer are responsible for the preparation of the financial statements and for being satisfied that they give a true and fair view. My responsibility is to audit, certify and report on the financial statements in accordance with the National Heritage Act 1983. I conducted my audit in accordance with International Standards on Auditing (UK and Ireland). Those standards require me and my staff to comply with the Auditing Practices Board's Ethical Standards for Auditors.

Scope of the Audit of the Financial Statements

An audit involves obtaining evidence about the amounts and disclosures in the financial statements sufficient to give reasonable assurance that the financial statements are free from material misstatement, whether caused by fraud or error. This includes an assessment of: whether the accounting policies are appropriate to HBMCE's and English Heritage's circumstances and have been consistently applied and adequately disclosed; the reasonableness of significant accounting estimates made by HBMCE and English Heritage and the overall presentation of the financial statements. In addition, I read all the financial and non-financial information in the Annual Report to identify material inconsistencies with the audited financial statements. If I become aware of any apparent material misstatements or inconsistencies I consider the implications for my certificate.

I am required to obtain evidence sufficient to give reasonable assurance that the expenditure and income reported in the financial statements have been applied to the purposes intended by Parliament and the financial transactions conform to the authorities which govern them.

Opinion on Regularity

In my opinion, in all material respects the expenditure and income have been applied to the purposes intended by Parliament and the financial transactions conform to the authorities which govern them.

Opinion on Financial Statements

In my opinion:

- the financial statements give a true and fair view of the state of HBMCE's and English Heritage's affairs as at 31 March 2012 and of its net expenditure for the year then ended; and

- the financial statements have been properly prepared in accordance with the National Heritage Act 1983 and Secretary of State directions issued thereunder.

The Certificate and Report of the Comptroller and Auditor General to the Houses of Parliament

Opinion on other matters

In my opinion:

- the part of the Remuneration Report to be audited has been properly prepared in accordance with the directions issued by the Secretary of State under the National Heritage Act 1983; and

- the information given in the Management Commentary, the Directors' Report, the Sustainability Report and English Heritage Key Performance Indicators included in the Annual Report for the financial year for which the financial statements are prepared is consistent with the financial statements.

Matters on which I report by exception

I have nothing to report in respect of the following matters which I report to you if, in my opinion:

- adequate accounting records have not been kept or returns adequate for my audit have not been received from branches not visited by my staff; or

- the financial statements and the part of the Remuneration Report to be audited are not in agreement with the accounting records or returns; or

- I have not received all of the information and explanations I require for my audit; or

- the Governance Statement does not reflect compliance with HM Treasury's guidance.

Report

I have no observations to make on these financial statements.

Amyas C E Morse
Comptroller and Auditor General
2 July 2012

National Audit Office
157-197 Buckingham Palace Road
Victoria
London
SW1W 9SP

Consolidated Statement of Comprehensive Net Expenditure for the Year Ended 31 March 2012

	Note	2011-2012 £'000	Restated 2010-2011 £'000
Income			
Earned Income	2	**52,107**	49,828
Other Operating Income	3	**1,861**	3,926
Investment Income	4	**230**	356
Total Income		**54,198**	54,110
Expenditure			
Grants	5	**31,375**	34,805
Heritage Protection and Planning	6	**32,665**	36,755
National Collections	7	**73,024**	73,954
Corporate and Support Services	8	**26,797**	30,504
Depreciation, Amortisation and Impairment	17, 18, 19	**6,222**	6,565
Total Expenditure		**170,083**	182,583
Net Expenditure for the Financial Year Before Exceptional Items		**(115,885)**	(128,473)
Restructuring and Relocation	9	**(2,534)**	(5,812)
Net Expenditure for the Financial Year After Exceptional Items		**(118,419)**	(134,285)
Transfer from/(to) the Development and Restricted Funds	32	**775**	(112)
Transfer from Revenue to Capital		**(1,083)**	-
Net Expenditure for the Financial Year		**(118,727)**	(134,397)
Other Comprehensive Expenditure			
Net Expenditure for the Year		**(118,727)**	(134,397)
Net Gain on Revaluation of Property, Plant and Equipment, Intangible Assets and Heritage Assets	17, 18, 19	**1,225**	11,137
Non-Government Capital Grant Funding and Donations	3	**2,855**	580
Net (Loss)/Gain in Revaluation of Investments	22b	**(8)**	21
Total Comprehensive Expenditure for the Financial Year		**(114,655)**	(122,659)

Consolidated Statement of Financial Position as at 31 March 2012

	Note	2012 £'000	Restated 2011 £'000	Restated 2010 £'000
Non-Current Assets				
Intangible Assets	17	1,378	809	980
Property, Plant & Equipment	18	67,211	62,787	59,313
Heritage Assets	19	22,551	23,308	17,856
Financial Assets	22b	-	448	427
Total Non-Current Assets		**91,140**	87,352	78,576
Current Assets				
Assets Classified as Held for Sale	23	832	-	-
Inventories	24	3,269	2,959	2,522
Trade and Other Receivables	25	10,983	11,220	14,593
Cash and Cash Equivalents	33	13,793	16,332	13,914
Total Current Assets		**28,877**	30,511	31,029
Total Assets		**120,017**	117,863	109,605
Current Liabilities				
Trade and Other Payables	28	(37,204)	(34,908)	(34,760)
Provisions	30	(840)	(5,041)	(2,804)
Obligations Under Finance Leases	27	(566)	(566)	(566)
Total Current Liabilities		**(38,610)**	(40,515)	(38,130)
Total Assets Less Current Liabilities		**81,407**	77,348	71,475
Non-Current Liabilities				
Other Payables	29	(3,150)	(3,081)	(3,017)
Provisions	30	(1,220)	(2,006)	(1,442)
Obligations Under Finance Leases	27	(6,887)	(6,903)	(6,919)
Total Non-Current Liabilities		**(11,257)**	(11,990)	(11,378)
Total Assets Less Liabilities		**70,150**	65,358	60,097
Taxpayers' Equity				
Revaluation Reserve	31	24,476	23,804	15,484
General Reserve	31	40,212	33,255	36,300
Development and Restricted Funds	32	5,022	7,851	7,886
Iveagh Bequest Capital Fund	22b, 37c	440	448	427
Total Reserves		**70,150**	65,358	60,097

The financial statements, which comprise the Statement of Comprehensive Net Expenditure, the Consolidated and HBMCE Statements of Financial Position, the Consolidated and HBMCE Statements of Cash Flows, the Consolidated and HBMCE Statements of Changes in Taxpayers' Equity and the related notes 1 to 39, were approved by the Commissioners of English Heritage and signed on their behalf on 27 June 2012 by:

Dr Simon Thurley
Chief Executive

Baroness Andrews OBE
Chair

ENGLISH HERITAGE ANNUAL REPORT AND ACCOUNTS 2011/12

HBMCE Statement of Financial Position as at 31 March 2012

	Note	2012 £'000	Restated 2011 £'000	Restated 2010 £'000
Non-Current Assets				
Intangible Assets	17	1,378	809	980
Property, Plant & Equipment	18	67,211	62,787	59,313
Heritage Assets	19	22,551	23,308	17,856
Financial Assets	22a	2,028	2,028	2,028
Total Non-Current Assets		**93,168**	88,932	80,177
Current Assets				
Assets Classified as Held for Sale	23	392	-	-
Inventories	24	-	66	46
Trade and Other Receivables	25	12,246	12,162	14,870
Cash and Cash Equivalents	33	13,292	15,831	13,412
Total Current Assets		**25,930**	28,059	28,328
Total Assets		**119,098**	116,991	108,505
Current Liabilities				
Trade and Other Payables	28	(36,755)	(34,535)	(34,087)
Provisions	30	(840)	(5,041)	(2,804)
Obligations Under Finance Leases	27	(566)	(566)	(566)
Total Current Liabilities		**(38,161)**	(40,142)	(37,457)
Total Assets Less Current Liabilities		**80,937**	76,849	71,048
Non-Current Liabilities				
Other Payables	29	(3,120)	(3,030)	(3,017)
Provisions	30	(1,220)	(2,006)	(1,442)
Obligations Under Finance Leases	27	(6,887)	(6,903)	(6,919)
Total Non-Current Liabilities		**(11,227)**	(11,939)	(11,378)
Total Assets Less Liabilities		**69,710**	64,910	59,670
Taxpayers' Equity				
Revaluation Reserve	31	24,476	23,804	15,484
General Reserve	31	40,212	33,255	36,300
Development and Restricted Funds	32	5,022	7,851	7,886
Total Reserves		**69,710**	64,910	59,670

The financial statements, which comprise the Statement of Comprehensive Net Expenditure, the Consolidated and HBMCE Statements of Financial Position, the Consolidated and HBMCE Statements of Cash Flows, the Consolidated and HBMCE Statements of Changes in Taxpayers' Equity and the related notes 1 to 39, were approved by the Commissioners of English Heritage and signed on their behalf on 27 June 2012 by:

Dr Simon Thurley
Chief Executive

Baroness Andrews OBE
Chair

Consolidated Statement of Cash Flows
for the Year Ended 31 March 2012

	Note	2011-2012 £'000	Restated 2010-2011 £'000
Cash Flows from Operating Activities			
Net Expenditure after Interest		**(118,419)**	(134,285)
Investment Income	4	**(230)**	(356)
Depreciation and Amortisation	17, 18, 19	**5,842**	5,295
Impairments and Profit on Disposal of Property, Plant & Equipment		**380**	1,241
Release from Capital Reserves		**453**	286
Increase in Inventories	24	**(310)**	(437)
Decrease in Trade and Other Receivables	25	**237**	3,373
(Decrease)/Increase in Trade and Other Payables		**(2,666)**	2,883
Net Cash Outflow from Operating Activities		**(114,713)**	(122,000)
Cash Flows from Investing Activities			
Interest Received		**206**	362
Dividends Received	37	**22**	22
Purchase of Property, Plant & Equipment and Heritage Assets	18, 19	**(8,814)**	(5,695)
Purchase of Intangible Assets	17	**(433)**	(124)
(Costs) on Disposal of Property, Plant & Equipment		**-**	(1)
Net Cash Outflow from Investing Activities		**(9,019)**	(5,436)
Cash Flows from Financing Activities			
Government Grant in Aid	31	121,193	129,854
Net Cash Inflow from Financing Activities		**121,193**	129,854
Net (Decrease)/Increase in Cash and Cash Equivalents		**(2,539)**	2,418
Cash and Cash Equivalents at the Beginning of the Year	33	16,332	13,914
Cash and Cash Equivalents at the End of the Year	33	**13,793**	16,332

HBMCE Statement of Cash Flows for the Year Ended 31 March 2012

	Note	2011-2012 £'000	Restated 2010-2011 £'000
Cash Flows from Operating Activities			
Net Expenditure after Interest		(118,419)	(134,285)
Investment Income		(225)	(351)
Depreciation and Amortisation	17, 18, 19	5,842	5,295
Impairments and Profit on Disposal of Property, Plant & Equipment		380	1,241
Release from Capital Reserves		453	287
Decrease/(Increase) in Inventories	24	66	(20)
Decrease/(Increase) in Trade and Other Receivables	25	(84)	2,708
(Decrease)/Increase in Trade and Other Payables		(2,721)	3,132
Net Cash Outflow from Operating Activities		**(114,708)**	(121,993)
Cash Flows from Investing Activities			
Interest Received		201	356
Dividends Received	37	22	22
Purchase of Property, Plant & Equipment and Heritage Assets	18, 19	(8,814)	(5,695)
Purchase of Intangible Assets	17	(433)	(124)
(Costs) on Disposal of Property, Plant & Equipment		-	(1)
Net Cash Outflow from Investing Activities		**(9,024)**	(5,442)
Cash Flows from Financing Activities			
Government Grant in Aid	31	121,193	129,854
Net Cash Inflow from Financing Activities		**121,193**	129,854
Net (Decrease)/Increase in Cash and Cash Equivalents		(2,539)	2,419
Cash and Cash Equivalents at the Beginning of the Year	33	15,831	13,412
Cash and Cash Equivalents at the End of the Year	33	**13,292**	15,831

Consolidated Statement of Changes in Taxpayers' Equity for the Year Ended 31 March 2012

	General Reserve £'000	Revaluation Reserve £'000	EU Government Grant Reserve £'000	Donated Asset Reserve £'000	Development and Restricted Funds £'000	Iveagh Bequest Capital Fund £'000	Total Reserves £'000
	Note 31	Note 31			Note 32	Note 37c	
Balance at 1 April 2010	23,536	14,285	1,876	13,386	7,886	427	61,396
Changes in Accounting Policy (IAS 8)	12,764	1,199	(1,876)	(13,386)	-	-	(1,299)
Restated Balance at 1 April 2010	36,300	15,484	-	-	7,886	427	60,097
Changes in Taxpayers' Equity for 2010/11 (Restated)							
Net Gain on Revaluation of Non-Current Assets	(558)	6,899	-	-	-	-	6,341
Net Gain on Revaluation of Investments	-	-	-	-	-	21	21
Release of Reserves to Net Expenditure	610	1,821	-	-	-	-	2,431
Expenditure for the Year	(134,397)	-	-	-	(1,006)	-	(135,403)
Transfer Between Reserves	400	(400)	-	-	-	-	-
Total Recognised Income and Expense for 2010/11 (Restated)	**(97,645)**	**23,804**	**-**	**-**	**6,880**	**448**	**(66,513)**
Grant in Aid Received	129,854	-	-	-	-	-	129,854
Other Income	1,046	-	-	-	971	-	2,017
Balance at 31 March 2011 (Restated)	**33,255**	**23,804**	**-**	**-**	**7,851**	**448**	**65,358**
Changes in Reserves for 2011/12							
Net Gain on Revaluation of Non-Current Assets	335	1,927	-	-	-	-	2,262
Net Loss on Revaluation of Investments	-	-	-	-	-	(8)	(8)
Release of Reserves to Net Expenditure	11	(394)	-	-	-	-	(383)
Expenditure for the Year	(118,727)	-	-	-	(3,165)	-	(121,892)
Transfer Between Reserves	861	(861)	-	-	-	-	-
Total Recognised Income and Expense for 2011/12	**(84,265)**	**24,476**	**-**	**-**	**4,686**	**440**	**(54,663)**
Grant in Aid Received	121,193	-	-	-	-	-	121,193
Other Income	3,284	-	-	-	336	-	3,620
Balance at 31 March 2012	**40,212**	**24,476**	**-**	**-**	**5,022**	**440**	**70,150**

HBMCE Statement of Changes in Taxpayers' Equity for the Year Ended 31 March 2012

	General Reserve £'000	Revaluation Reserve £'000	EU Government Grant Reserve £'000	Donated Asset Reserve £'000	Development and Restricted Funds £'000	Total Reserves £'000
	Note 31	Note 31			Note 32	
Balance at 1 April 2010	23,536	14,285	1,876	13,386	7,886	60,969
Changes in Accounting Policy (IAS 8)	12,764	1,199	(1,876)	(13,386)	-	(1,299)
Restated Balance at 1 April 2010	36,300	15,484	-	-	7,886	59,670
Changes in Taxpayers' Equity for 2010/11 (Restated)						
Net Gain/(Loss) on Revaluation of Non-Current Assets	(558)	6,899	-	-	-	6,341
Release of Reserves to Net Expenditure	610	1,821	-	-	-	2,431
Expenditure for the Year	(134,397)	-	-	-	(1,006)	(135,403)
Transfer Between Reserves	400	(400)	-	-	-	-
Total Recognised Income and Expense for 2010/11 (Restated)	(97,645)	23,804	-	-	6,880	(66,961)
Grant in Aid Received	129,854	-	-	-	-	129,854
Other Income	1,046	-	-	-	971	2,017
Balance at 31 March 2011 (Restated)	33,255	23,804	-	-	7,851	64,910
Changes in Reserves for 2011/12						
Net Gain on Revaluation of Non-Current Assets	335	1,927	-	-	-	2,262
Release of Reserves to Net Expenditure	11	(394)	-	-	-	(383)
Expenditure for the Year	(118,727)	-	-	-	(3,165)	(121,892)
Transfer Between Reserves	861	(861)	-	-	-	-
Total Recognised Income and Expense for 2011/12	(84,265)	24,476	-	-	4,686	(55,103)
Grant in Aid Received	121,193	-	-	-	-	121,193
Other Income	3,284	-	-	-	336	3,620
Balance at 31 March 2012	40,212	24,476	-	-	5,022	69,710

Notes to the Financial Statements

1 Statement of Accounting Policies

a) Accounting Convention

The financial statements have been prepared in accordance with the 2011-2012 Government Financial Reporting Manual (FReM) issued by HM Treasury. The accounting policies contained in the FReM apply International Financial Reporting Standards (IFRS) as adapted or interpreted for the public sector context. Where the FReM permits a choice of accounting policy, the accounting policy which is judged to be most appropriate to the particular circumstances of English Heritage for the purpose of giving a true and fair view has been selected. The particular policies adopted by English Heritage are described below. They have been applied consistently in dealing with items that are considered material to the accounts.

The financial statements have been prepared under the historical cost convention, modified for the revaluation of property, plant and machinery, IT equipment, furniture and fittings, intangible assets, heritage assets and inventories where material.

English Heritage Trading Limited, a subsidiary undertaking of HBMCE, continued trading throughout the year ended 31 March 2012. HBMCE is the Administrative Trustee of the Iveagh Bequest. Hence the financial statements include a consolidation of HBMCE, English Heritage Trading Limited and the Iveagh Bequest.

b) Value Added Tax

Income is shown net of Value Added Tax. Expenditure is shown inclusive of any non-recoverable VAT incurred.

c) Membership Income

Annual membership income is recognised in the Statement of Comprehensive Net Expenditure to match the benefit provided to the member. Income received that relates to benefits to be provided in the following year is treated as Deferred Income on the Statement of Financial Position. Life membership income is released to the Statement of Comprehensive Net Expenditure over 25 years.

d) Admission, Retail and Other Earned Income

Admission, retail and other earned income is recognised when earned.

e) Government Grant in Aid Receivable

Parliamentary grant is voted to meet English Heritage's cash payments falling due during the financial year. English Heritage accounts for its expenditure on an accruals basis, thus incurring liabilities during a year which may not need to be satisfied by cash payments until future financial years.

Government Grant in Aid receivable is credited to the General Reserve (note 31).

f) Other Grants Receivable

Other grants receivable are recognised in the Statement of Comprehensive Net Expenditure when the conditions of the grant have been fulfilled and the grant is claimable. If such a grant is subject to a condition, the grant will be deferred until such time as the condition has been fulfilled.

g) Grants Payable

Grants payable to individuals and bodies by English Heritage in accordance with its statutory powers and duties are accounted for when the grant recipient carries out the specific activity which forms the basis of entitlement. Grant offers made yet to become payable are quantified at note 34a.

Where grants have been offered but not paid, an accrual of grant owing is calculated based on the stage of completion of the works. For grant schemes where grants are payable in advance, an estimate of the prepayment made is calculated based on works not yet complete.

Notes to the Financial Statements

1 Statement of Accounting Policies

h) Intangible Assets

Licences to use software purchased from third parties with a life of more than one year are shown on the Statement of Financial Position as Non-Current Intangible Assets and amortised over the life of the licence or the life of the related asset where there is no licence expiry date. Annual licences to use software are charged to the Statement of Comprehensive Net Expenditure as they are incurred.

Systems development is capitalised and amortised over its useful economic life.

Expenditure on developing the English Heritage brand is charged to the Statement of Comprehensive Net Expenditure as it is incurred.

i) Property, Plant and Equipment

Operational Land & Buildings and Dwellings

Land and buildings owned by, or in the guardianship of, English Heritage are treated as Non-Current Assets in accordance with the FReM and are classified as either:

- Pure heritage assets (non-operational heritage assets);
- Operational heritage assets; or
- Operational (non-heritage) assets, held within Property, Plant and Equipment.

The policy on heritage assets is disclosed at note 1j.

Operational heritage land and buildings which, in addition to being held by English Heritage in pursuit of its overall objectives, are also used for revenue generating or other non-heritage purposes, are professionally valued and held on the Statement of Financial Position within Heritage Assets. The valuation method used depends upon the type of building, its use and any conditions attached to its disposal.

Operational (non-heritage) land and buildings are professionally valued and held on the Statement of Financial Position within Property, Plant and Equipment. The valuation method used depends upon the type of building, its use and any conditions attached to its disposal.

Mixed use buildings are classified according to the majority use. Classification and valuations of vacant properties are informed by the type of building and its intended future use.

With the exception of major refurbishments and items with a net book value of less than £50,000, all land and buildings held on the Statement of Financial Position are subject to a full professional valuation every five years. Major refurbishments are not valued as they are indistinguishable from the underlying asset. They are depreciated over a shorter useful economic life than the underlying asset. Assets with a value of less than £50,000 are revalued with reference to relevant indices published by the Building Cost Information Services as at 31 March. A full quinquennial revaluation was undertaken as at 31 March 2011 by professionally qualified internal valuers, and the following external valuers: Ash & Co, Bare Leaning and Bare, Bidwells, Brownhill Vickers, Carter Jonas, Edwin Thompson, Humberts Leisure, King Sturge, Kivells, Mildred Howells, Powis Hughes, RNJ Partnership, Turner and Holman, the Valuation Office Agency and Walton Goddland, in accordance with Royal Institution of Chartered Surveyors' guidance. Interim valuations were undertaken by Mildred Howells, RNJ Partnership, Powis Hughes and Turner and Holman during the financial year ended 31 March 2012.

The values of the land and buildings held as Non-Current Assets are reviewed annually using relevant indices published by the Building Cost Information Services as at 31 March. Any change in value is reflected in the relevant reserve.

Where possible, assets are valued at fair value. Where there is no available market information due to the specialised nature of the asset, depreciated replacement cost valuation is used.

Any unrealised gain on revaluation at the Statement of Financial Position date is taken directly to the Revaluation Reserve.

Notes to the Financial Statements

1 Statement of Accounting Policies

Unrealised losses at the date of the Statement of Financial Position are written off against the proportion of the credit balance on the reserve which relates to the assets concerned. Any other unrealised losses are charged to the Statement of Comprehensive Net Expenditure.

Plant & Machinery, IT and Furniture & Fittings

Plant and machinery, IT equipment, furniture and fittings are initially recorded in the Statement of Financial Position at cost. Subsequent expenditure is recorded on the Statement of Financial Position if the expenditure enhances the economic benefits of the asset.

These assets are reviewed annually to ensure that the carrying value remains appropriate. Revaluation and impairment adjustments are made where the adjustment is material.

Assets Under Construction

Assets under construction comprise expenditure on the creation or enhancement of Non-Current Assets not brought into use at the Statement of Financial Position date. Transfers are made from assets under construction to the relevant category of Non-Current Asset when the asset is brought into use.

j) Heritage Assets

English Heritage has two classes of heritage assets which are held in pursuit of its overall objectives in relation to the enjoyment and preservation of heritage. The classes are accounted for as follows:

Land and Buildings - Pure Heritage Assets (non-operational heritage assets) and Operational Heritage Assets

English Heritage maintains over 550 pure heritage land and building assets at over 400 sites throughout England. English Heritage does not consider that reliable cost or valuation information can be obtained for the vast majority of items held as heritage land and buildings as, owing to the incomparable nature of many of the assets, conventional valuation approaches lack sufficient reliability and that, even if valuations could be obtained, the costs would be onerous compared with the additional benefits derived by English Heritage and the users of the accounts. English Heritage does not therefore recognise those assets on its Statement of Financial Position, other than recent acquisitions where a reliable valuation is possible. Expenditure on these assets, where it does not result in the creation of a new operational heritage asset, is charged to the Statement of Comprehensive Net Expenditure as it is incurred.

All operational heritage assets are capitalised on the Statement of Financial Position in accordance with note 1i.

Heritage Artefacts and Archives

English Heritage maintains over 500,000 heritage artefacts in its collection and almost 12 million archive records in its archive. English Heritage does not consider that reliable cost or valuation information can be obtained for the vast majority of items held in the artefacts collection and archives and that, even if valuations could be obtained, the costs would be onerous compared with the additional benefits derived by English Heritage and the users of the accounts. This is because of the diverse nature of the assets held, the number of assets held and the lack of comparable market values. English Heritage therefore does not recognise these assets on its Statement of Financial Position, other than those additions to collections and archives acquired after 1 April 2001 and recognised as per previous requirements of the Government Financial Reporting Manual. These items are recognised at cost or, where donated, at current market value.

Expenditure which, in English Heritage's view, is required to preserve or clearly prevent further deterioration of individual collection and archive items is recognised in the Statement of Comprehensive Net Expenditure as it is incurred.

Further information on the acquisition, disposal, management and preservation of English Heritage's heritage assets is given in notes 19, 20 and 21 to the accounts.

Notes to the Financial Statements

1 Statement of Accounting Policies

k) Donated Assets

Assets donated by third parties, either by gift of the asset or by way of funds for the asset, will be treated as Non-Current Assets and held at current value on receipt.

Donated assets are revalued in the same way as other Non-Current Assets.

l) Depreciation and Amortisation

Depreciation is provided on property, plant and machinery, IT equipment, furniture and fittings (excluding land and assets under construction) and amortisation is provided on software licences and systems development, in equal amounts each year in order to write down their cost to their estimated residual value over their anticipated useful economic lives. These are as follows:

Intangible Assets

Software licences	4-10 years
Systems development	4-10 years

Purchased goodwill and intangible assets under construction are not amortised. Purchased goodwill is subject to an annual impairment review.

Tangible Assets

Non-heritage buildings and gardens

- Dwellings	50 years
- Other permanent or brick/stone buildings	50 years
- Non brick/stone visitor centres, shops, museums, exhibition buildings	25-40 years
- Other non brick/stone structures	20 years
- Paths, car parks, playgrounds	20-25 years
- Gardens	50 years

Refurbishments

- Shop/café/holiday cottage refurbishment, infrastructure	10-20 years
Plant and machinery	5-15 years
IT, furniture and fittings	4-10 years

Assets held under finance leases are depreciated over the term of the relevant lease.

When considering anticipated useful economic lives, regard is given to the IAS 16 requirement to identify assets which have distinct major components with substantially different useful economic lives. Where such assets are identified, separate useful economic lives for component assets are considered.

Operational and pure heritage buildings and historic artefacts and archives are not depreciated, as they are deemed to have indefinite lives.

m) Financial Assets

Non-Current Financial Assets, other than those in subsidiary undertakings are held at fair value. Any unrealised gain at the Statement of Financial Position date is taken directly to reserves.

Unrealised losses at the Statement of Financial Position date are written off against the proportion of credit balance on the Capital Fund which relates to the investment concerned. Any other unrealised losses are charged to the Statement of Comprehensive Net Expenditure.

Investments in subsidiary undertakings are held at cost.

Current Financial Assets consist of funds other than Cash and Cash Equivalents held on deposit for a period of between three and six months, in accordance with English Heritage's treasury policy.

Notes to the Financial Statements

1 Statement of Accounting Policies

n) Non-Current Assets Held for Sale

The value of Non-Current Assets held for sale is measured at the lower of their carrying amount and fair value less costs to sell. Assets classified as held for sale are not depreciated. In order to be classified as held for sale, a Non-Current Asset must meet the criteria specified within IFRS 5.

o) Inventories

Goods held for resale are stated at the lower of current replacement cost and net realisable value. Origination costs of internally produced publications for resale are written off over the first print run.

p) Leases

Finance Leases

Assets held under finance leases are recognised as assets of English Heritage at their fair value or, if lower, at the present value of the minimum lease payments, each determined at the inception of the lease. The corresponding liability to the lessor is included in the Statement of Financial Position as a finance lease obligation. Lease payments are apportioned between finance charges and the reduction of the lease obligation so as to achieve a consistent rate of interest on the remaining balance of the liability. Finance charges are charged directly against income.

Contingent rentals are recognised directly in the Statement of Comprehensive Net Expenditure when they are incurred.

Operating Leases

Operating lease costs are charged to the Statement of Comprehensive Net Expenditure as incurred.

q) Cash and Cash Equivalents

Cash comprises cash on hand and demand deposits. Cash equivalents are investments with a short term maturity of less than three months from the date of acquisition. Cash which is surplus to immediate cash flow requirements is placed on deposit in accordance with English Heritage's treasury policy.

r) Pension Costs

English Heritage is a member of the Principal Civil Service Pension Scheme (PCSPS). This is a multi-employer defined benefit scheme. English Heritage also operates a by-analogy scheme to the PCSPS for the previous Chairmen. Both schemes satisfy the requirements of applicable accounting standards (see note 16).

s) Restricted and Development Funds

Funds held by English Heritage that can only be applied for particular purposes imposed by donors are held as restricted and development funds. Investments to cover the amounts held in restricted funds are placed on deposit at fixed rates of interest for periods of up to six months in accordance with English Heritage's treasury policy and are treated as Cash and Cash Equivalents or Current Financial Assets in line with accounting policies 1m and 1q.

In accordance with the provisions of the FReM, the Restricted and Development Funds have been accounted for in line with the Charities' Statement of Recommended Practice.

t) Segmental Reporting

The primary format used for segmental reporting is by expenditure type as this reflects English Heritage's internal management structure and reporting. English Heritage's assets and liabilities are shared across the operating segments and consequently it is not possible to separately identify which segment they relate to, in line with the IFRS 8 exemption.

The segments reported reflect the management structure reported internally within English Heritage on a monthly basis.

Notes to the Financial Statements

1 Statement of Accounting Policies

Heritage Protection and Planning is responsible for heritage protection, strategy, research, advising on making and managing changes to historic places and publishing the annual *Heritage at Risk Register*. National Collections is responsible for English Heritage's properties, marketing, capital development, commercial activities, fundraising, education, conservation, properties presentation, publishing and the English Heritage Archive. Corporate and Support Services are responsible for advising government and other bodies on the value of our historic environment and includes national advice, communications, legal services and corporate governance; and also for providing a range of services to the organisation including finance, human resources, IT and procurement.

u) Provisions

Provisions are made where the conditions for such a liability exist at the Statement of Financial Position date which can be reliably estimated. Balances that are not payable within one year of the balance sheet date are discounted to reflect future cash flows in current year prices, where the time value of money is material. The discount rate is set by HM Treasury and is currently 2.8% for pension provisions.

v) Impact of New and Updated Financial Reporting Standards and Interpretations

Adopted for 2011-2012

The following new IFRS and FRS and revised or amended IFRS and FRS were incorporated into the Government Financial Reporting Manual and adopted by English Heritage from 1 April 2011.

The primary financial statements and related notes have been restated retrospectively as a result of the change in accounting for non-government grants and donations introduced into the FReM during 2011-2012. This change requires English Heritage to recognise all grant and donation income (other than Grant In Aid) as income in the Statement of Comprehensive Net Expenditure in the year in which it was received (unless a condition attached to that grant has been met, in which case the income should be deferred until all conditions have been met).

There are no standards and interpretations in issue but not yet adopted by English Heritage that the directors anticipate will have a material effect on the reported income or net assets of English Heritage.

w) Significant Accounting Estimates and Judgements

Key sources of estimation uncertainty and judgements made in applying accounting policy exist in estimations of the stage of completion for grant accruals and prepayments as well as in provisions for future liabilities for early retirement and redundancy costs.

2 Earned Income

	2011-2012 £'000	2010-2011 £'000
Admission Income	15,383	14,287
Retail and Catering Income	12,652	12,077
Membership Income	19,677	18,802
Other Earned Income	4,395	4,662
Total Earned Income	**52,107**	49,828

Notes to the Financial Statements

3 Other Operating Income

	2011-2012 Capital £'000	2011-2012 Revenue £'000	Restated 2010-2011 Capital £'000	Restated 2010-2011 Revenue £'000
Grants Receivable				
European Community	-	125	-	8
Heritage Lottery Fund	657	785	-	542
Aggregates Levy	-	-	-	1,012
Other	30	435	242	1,113
Total Grants Receivable	687	1,345	242	2,675
Transfer from Capital Reserves	-	47	-	25
Transfer from Deferred Income	261	-	-	-
Total Grants	**948**	**1,392**	242	2,700
Donations	2,053	279	658	1,088
Transfer from Capital Reserves	-	136	-	124
Transfer to Deferred Income	(146)	-	(320)	-
Other Operating Income	-	54	-	14
Total Other Operating Income	**2,855**	**1,861**	580	3,926
Non-government grant funding recognised in Statement of Comprehensive Net Expenditure	(948)	948	(242)	242
Donations recognised in Statement of Comprehensive Net Expenditure	(1,907)	1,907	(338)	338
Non-Government Capital Grant Funding and Donations	**(2,855)**	**2,855**	(580)	580

4 Investment Income

	2011-2012 £'000	2010-2011 £'000
Interest Receivable	208	334
Dividends Receivable	22	22
Total Investment Income	**230**	356

Notes to the Financial Statements

5 Grants

	2011-2012 £'000	2010-2011 £'000
Buildings and Monuments	11,196	12,306
Conservation Areas	2,277	2,911
Cathedrals	31	181
Other Places of Worship	7,150	8,699
Historic Environment	5,075	5,711
Aggregates Levy Historic Environment	-	905
Other	5,646	4,092
Total Grants Payable	**31,375**	34,805

6 Heritage Protection and Planning

	2011-2012 £'000	2010-2011 £'000
Designation and Listing	4,510	4,993
Heritage Protection	12,295	12,184
Managing the Historic Environment	15,860	19,578
Total Heritage Protection and Planning	**32,665**	36,755

7 National Collections

	2011-2012 £'000	2010-2011 £'000
Running the Properties	40,930	40,797
Caring for our Collections	31,529	32,232
Development and Fundraising	565	925
Total National Collections	**73,024**	73,954

8 Corporate and Support Services

	2011-2012 £'000	2010-2011 £'000
National Advice and Information	3,012	3,715
Governance and Legal Services	1,693	3,368
Finance	1,778	2,320
Information Systems	10,849	12,298
Human Resources	1,889	1,981
Office Costs	7,576	6,822
Total Corporate and Support Services	**26,797**	30,504

9 Restructuring and Relocation Costs

In 2010/11 English Heritage began a restructuring programme to reduce costs in future years to allow it to operate within its reduced Grant in Aid. Costs incurred during the financial year ended 31 March 2012 were £2,534,000 (2011: £5,812,000).

Notes to the Financial Statements

10 Taxation

HBMCE enjoys the status of a charity for taxation purposes. No taxation liability is expected on its operations for the year ended 31 March 2012 (2011: nil). English Heritage Trading Limited transferred all its profits for the year ended 31 March 2012 (2011: all) to HBMCE under the Gift Aid rules. Hence, it suffered nil taxation charge (2011: nil) as it had no taxable profits.

11 Auditor's Fees

	2011-2012 £'000	2010-2011 £'000
Auditor's remuneration and expenses for statutory audit work:		
English Heritage and HBMCE	63	60
English Heritage Trading Limited	8	8
Total Auditor's Fees	**71**	68

The fee for 2011/12 includes £3,000 relating to additional audit work required for the quinquennial valuation in 2010/11. During the year English Heritage has not purchased any non-audit services from its auditor, the National Audit Office (2011: nil).

12 Commissioners

Commissioners' emoluments totalled £103,000 (2011: £107,000) and wholly related to basic fees in respect of their duties as Commissioners and as members of advisory committees and panels. Emoluments also include any income tax payable on home to office travel expenses which English Heritage pays on the Commissioners' behalf. No Commissioner received any performance related fees. The Chair, Baroness Andrews OBE, is the highest paid Commissioner and her emoluments for the year were £51,000 (2011: £51,000). This position is non-pensionable.

The emoluments of the other Commissioners were as follows:	2011-2012 £'000	2010-2011 £'000
Ms Lynda Addison OBE	6	4
Ms Maria Adebowale (term of appointment ended 31 August 2011)	2	4
Mrs Joyce Bridges CBE (term of appointment ended 31 August 2011)	4	10
Mr Manish Chande (term of appointment ended 31 August 2011)	2	4
Professor Sir Barry Cunliffe CBE	8	8
Mr Peter Draper (appointed 1 September 2011)	2	-
Mr David Fursdon	4	4
Professor Ronald Hutton	5	4
Mr Michael Jolly CBE (term of appointment ended 29 September 2010)	-	2
Ms Jane Kennedy	4	4
Vice Admiral Sir Tim Laurence KCVO CB ADC (appointed 1 September 2011)	2	-
Mr Martin Moore (appointed 1 September 2011)	2	-
Mr Graham Morrison (appointed 1 September 2011)	2	-
Mr John Walker CBE	4	4
Mr Chris Wilkinson OBE RA (term of appointment ended 8 July 2011)	1	4
Ms Elizabeth Williamson (term of appointment ended 31 August 2011)	2	4
Baroness Young of Hornsey OBE (appointed 1 September 2011)	2	-

All current Commissioners have been appointed for fixed terms of 4 years, the appointments are non-pensionable. Commissioners' emoluments are set by the Department for Culture, Media and Sport.

Notes to the Financial Statements

13 Advisory Committee and Panel Members

English Heritage has a number of Advisory Committees and Panels which report directly to Commission. Advisory Committee and Panel Members who were not Commissioners received emoluments of £4,000 during the year (2011: nil).

14 Related Party Transactions and Connected Bodies

Connected Bodies

English Heritage is sponsored by the Department for Culture, Media and Sport (DCMS) which is regarded as a related party. There were material transactions with DCMS in respect of the receipt of Grant in Aid (note 31).

There were also material transactions with the following entities for which DCMS is regarded as the parent department:

Arts Council England
British Broadcasting Corporation
British Museum
Imperial War Museum
National Heritage Memorial Fund

National Museums Liverpool
National Portrait Gallery
Visit Britain
Victoria and Albert Museum

During the year English Heritage had material transactions with the following Government Departments and Central Government bodies:

Biotechnology and Biological Sciences Research Council
Cabinet Office
Department for the Environment, Food & Rural Affairs (Defra)
Department for Work and Pensions (DWP)
Gloucester Heritage Urban Regeneration Company Ltd
Natural England
Rural Payments Agency

Material Transactions with Related Party Interests

During the year English Heritage had the following material transactions in which there was a related interest:

- Ms Lynda Addison OBE, a Commissioner, is a trustee and director of the Town and Country Planning Association which received £3,000 for subscription to the National Planning Forum for 2011/12.

- The brother of Ms Maria Adebowale, a Commissioner, is a member of the House of Lords as are Baroness Young of Hornsey, a Commissioner, and Baroness Andrews, Chair. The House of Lords received £1,000 for Commissioners' meetings.

- Professor Sir Barry Cunliffe CBE, a Commissioner, is a trustee of The English Heritage Foundation along with Dr Simon Thurley, Chief Executive, who is also their Company Secretary. English Heritage have an outstanding receivable of £122,000 owed by the Foundation in respect of management services.

Notes to the Financial Statements

14 Related Party Transactions and Connected Bodies

- Mr David Fursdon, a Commissioner, is a Committee Member for the Duchy of Cornwall Rural Committee. The Committee paid rent totalling £2,000 and received rent payments from English Heritage of £1,000. He is also a Board Member for The Crown Estate. The Crown Estate received £181,000 of grant payments. In addition, £2,000 of lease payments were made to, and £50,000 of payments were received from, The Crown Estate. He is also a consultant to Smiths Gore who received £7,000 of lease payments.

- Ms Jane Kennedy, a Commissioner, is a partner of Purcell Miller Tritton Architects which received fee payments totalling £231,000 and have an outstanding payables balance of £1,000. She is also a member of the Peterborough Cathedral Fabric Advisory Committee who received a grant of £5,000. Her husband is a member of the Society of Antiquaries Kelmscott Manor Management Advisory Committee. The Society of Antiquaries received £3,000 of payments for room hire.

- Mr Martin Moore, a Commisioner, is Managing Director of Prudential Property Investment Managers Ltd (PRUPIM) who received payments of £1,066,000 for building rental services. He is also a director of M&G Investment Management Ltd who are responsible for the investment decisions of Charifund. Charifund is an equity investment fund within which the funds of the Iveagh Bequest have been invested.

- Mr Graham Morrison, a Commisioner, is a partner in Allies and Morrison who received research fees of £12,000.

- Mrs Magdalen Fisher, Development Director, is a trustee of St Gabriel's Parish House in the same parish as St Gabriel's Church which received a grant of £28,000.

- Dr Edward Impey, Director of Heritage Protection and Planning, is a trustee of The Ancient Monuments Society who received payments totalling £57,000, including £56,000 of grants.

- Mrs Shirley Jackson, Retail Director, is a trustee of the Association for Cultural Enterprises, who received payments of £1,000.

- Dr Anna Keay, Curatorial Director, is a trustee of the Landmark Trust who received grant payments totalling £131,000.

- Mr Mark Pemberton, the Director of National Collections, is a trustee of Wedgwood Museum's Trust. Wedgwood Museum Trading Ltd received a grant of £49,000.

- The partner of Miss Carol Pyrah, North East Planning Regional Director, runs a research consultancy business which has received payments totalling £15,000 for research projects commissioned by English Heritage.

- Mr Tim Reeve, Historic Properties Director, is a trustee of the Hadrian's Wall Trust (formerly Hadrian's Wall Heritage Ltd) who received £204,000 including £203,000 of grant payments. He is also Board Director of the Association of Leading Visitor Attractions (ALVA) who received £4,000 for market research services.

- The partner of Mr Chris Smith, National Planning Director, is a trustee of the Council for British Archaeology who received payments of £462,000 including various grant payments totalling £459,000.

- Dr Simon Thurley, Chief Executive, is an advisory board member of the Institute for Medieval and Renaissance Studies, Durham University. Durham University received grant payments of £6,000 and payments of £7,000 for archaeological works. He is also a trustee of the Canal and River Trust. The Canal and River Trust will commence operations in 2012 and is a merger of British Waterways and The Waterways Trust. The Waterways Trust received a grant for £25,000. A grant of £2,000 was also made to British Waterways.

No other Commissioners, key managerial staff or other related party have undertaken any material related party transactions with English Heritage during the year.

Notes to the Financial Statements

15 Employees

a) Employee Numbers

The average number of persons employed during the year expressed as full-time equivalents was:

	2011-2012	2010-2011
National Collections	1,076	1,123
Heritage Protection and Planning	572	641
Corporate and Support Services	240	249
Total Employee Numbers	**1,888**	2,013

Employee numbers include 19 agency staff (2011: 17). Included within the above numbers are 11 staff who have been engaged on capitalised projects (2011: 4) whose costs have been capitalised.

b) Employee costs

	2011-2012 £'000	2010-2011 £'000
Wages and Salaries	52,906	56,587
Social Security Costs	3,993	4,284
Pension Costs	8,987	9,729
Redundancy and Severance Costs	2,534	6,382
Agency Staff Costs	646	695
Total Employee Costs	**69,066**	77,677

Included within the above costs are £454,000 wages and salaries costs (2011: £315,000), £37,000 social security costs (2011: £27,000) and £60,000 pension costs (2011: £45,000) that have been capitalised within Non-Current Assets (notes 17, 18 and 19). There are nil redundancy and severance costs (2011: nil) and £5,000 agency staff costs (2011: nil) that have been capitalised.

c) Reporting of Civil Service and Other Compensation Schemes - Exit Packages

	Number of Compulsory Redundancies		Number of Other Agreed Departures		Total Number of Exit Packages	
	2011-2012	2010-2011	2011-2012	2010-2011	2011-2012	2010-2011
Less than £10,000	70	2	14	10	84	12
£10,000 to £25,000	98	12	40	1	138	13
£25,000 to £50,000	47	8	20	3	67	11
£50,000 to £100,000	16	2	8	3	24	5
£100,000 to £150,000	1	1	-	2	1	3
Greater than £150,000	1	2	-	-	1	2
Total Number of Exit Packages	233	27	82	19	315	46
Total Resource Cost (£'000)	**4,921**	1,407	**2,033**	669	**6,954**	2,076

Redundancy and other departure costs have been paid in accordance with the provisions of the Civil Service Compensation Scheme, a statutory scheme made under the Superannuation Act 1972. Exit costs are accounted for in full in the year of departure. Where the department has agreed early retirements, the additional costs are met by the department and not by the Civil Service pension scheme. Ill-health retirement costs are met by the pension scheme and are not included in the table.

Notes to the Financial Statements

16 Pension Costs

English Heritage is a member of the Principal Civil Service Pension Scheme (PCSPS). As the PCSPS is an unfunded multi-employer defined benefit scheme, English Heritage is unable to identify its share of the underlying assets and liabilities. A full actuarial valuation was carried out as at 31 March 2007. Details can be found in the resource accounts of the Cabinet Office: Civil Superannuation (www.civilservice.gov.uk/my-civil-service/pensions).

For the year ended 31 March 2012, employers' contributions were payable to the PCSPS at 1 of 4 rates in the range 16.7% to 24.3% of pensionable pay, based on salary bands (2011: 16.7% to 24.3%). The Scheme Actuary reviews employer contributions usually every 4 years following a full scheme valuation. The contribution rates are set to meet the cost of the benefits accruing during the year ended 31 March 2012 to be paid when the member retires and not the benefits paid during this period to existing pensioners.

Total employer contributions to the PCSPS were £8,763,000 (2011: £9,628,000).

Employees joining English Heritage after 1 October 2002 can opt to open a partnership pension account, a stakeholder pension with an employer contribution. Employer's contributions of £167,000 were paid to a panel of 3 appointed stakeholder pension providers (2011: £178,000). Employer contributions are age-related and range from 3% to 12.5% of pensionable pay. Employers also match employee contributions up to 3% of pensionable pay. In addition, employer contributions of £6,000 (2011: £7,000), 0.8% of pensionable pay, were payable to the PCSPS to cover the cost of the future provision of lump sum benefits on death in service and ill health retirement of these employees.

Contributions due to the partnership pension providers at the Statement of Financial Position date were nil (2011: nil). Contributions prepaid at that date were nil (2011: nil).

English Heritage operates a by-analogy scheme to the PCSPS for 3 of the previous chairmen. The scheme liability at 31 March 2012 was £230,000 (2011: £226,000). This scheme has been valued by the Government Actuary's Department in accordance with Treasury guidelines and IAS 19 principles.

Notes to the Financial Statements

17 Intangible Assets

	Software Licences £'000	Systems Development £'000	Goodwill £'000	Assets Under Construction £'000	Total £'000
English Heritage and HBMCE					
Cost or Valuation					
At 1 April 2011	1,066	11,220	104	-	12,390
Additions	157	-	-	276	433
Reclassifications	31	-	-	(31)	-
Indexation	1	12	-	-	13
Revaluations	-	885	-	-	885
At 31 March 2012	1,255	12,117	104	245	**13,721**
Amortisation					
At 1 April 2011	886	10,662	33	-	11,581
Charged in year	109	267	-	-	376
Indexation	1	12	-	-	13
Revaluations	-	380	-	-	380
Write-back Amortisation	-	-	(7)	-	(7)
At 31 March 2012	996	11,321	26	-	**12,343**
Carrying amount at 31 March 2011	180	558	71	-	809
Carrying amount at 31 March 2012	259	796	78	245	1,378

All intangible assets are owned by English Heritage (2011: all).

Notes to the Financial Statements

17 Intangible Assets

	Software Licences £'000	Systems Development £'000	Goodwill £'000	Assets Under Construction £'000	Total £'000
English Heritage and HBMCE					
Cost or Valuation					
At 1 April 2010	1,143	12,146	104	139	13,532
Additions	62	-	-	328	390
Disposals	(94)	-	-	-	(94)
Reclassifications	62	405	-	(467)	-
Revaluations	(107)	(1,331)	-	-	(1,438)
At 31 March 2011	1,066	11,220	104	-	**12,390**
Amortisation					
At 1 April 2010	978	11,541	33	-	12,552
Charged in year	91	384		-	475
Disposals	(94)	-	-	-	(94)
Impairments	10	22	-	-	32
Revaluations	(99)	(1,285)	-	-	(1,384)
At 31 March 2011	886	10,662	33	-	**11,581**
Carrying amount at 31 March 2010	165	605	71	139	980
Carrying amount at 31 March 2011	**180**	**558**	**71**	**-**	**809**

Notes to the Financial Statements

18 Property, Plant & Equipment

	Operational Land & Buildings £'000	Dwellings £'000	Plant & Machinery £'000	IT £'000	Furniture & Fittings £'000	Assets under Construction £'000	Total £'000
English Heritage and HBMCE							
Cost or Valuation							
At 1 April 2011	66,192	4,157	8,357	4,714	4,460	5,503	93,383
Additions	-	-	256	-	-	8,377	8,633
Disposals	-	-	(88)	(53)	-	-	(141)
Impairments	(207)	(11)	(42)	-	(201)	-	(461)
Reclassifications	6,375	188	661	-	-	(6,700)	524
Indexation	(182)	-	(10)	5	(100)	-	(287)
Revaluations	(1,025)	-	22	-	-	-	(1,003)
At 31 March 2012	**71,153**	**4,334**	**9,156**	**4,666**	**4,159**	**7,180**	**100,648**
Depreciation							
At 1 April 2011	18,850	869	5,611	2,814	2,452	-	30,596
Charged in year	3,264	52	794	502	498	-	5,110
Disposals	-	-	(88)	(53)	-	-	(141)
Impairments	(12)	(12)	(22)	-	(97)	-	(143)
Indexation	(107)	-	(16)	3	(99)	-	(219)
Revaluations	(1,727)	-	4	-	-	-	(1,723)
Write-back Depreciation	(24)	3	(22)	-	-	-	(43)
At 31 March 2012	**20,244**	**912**	**6,261**	**3,266**	**2,754**	**-**	**33,437**
Carrying amount at 31 March 2011	47,342	3,288	2,746	1,900	2,008	5,503	62,787
Carrying amount at 31 March 2012	**50,909**	**3,422**	**2,895**	**1,400**	**1,405**	**7,180**	**67,211**
Asset financing:							
Owned	39,637	3,422	2,895	1,400	1,405	7,180	55,939
Finance Leased	11,272	-	-	-	-	-	11,272
Carrying amount at 31 March 2012	**50,909**	**3,422**	**2,895**	**1,400**	**1,405**	**7,180**	**67,211**

Total Non-Current Asset acquisitions in the year to the fair value of £5,927,000 were funded by government grant (2011: £4,414,000), £296,000 by non-government grant (2011: £235,000), £2,193,000 by donations (2011: £345,000) and £871,000 by lottery funding (2011: nil).

The transfers from Assets under Construction to other Non-Current Asset categories represent Assets under Construction which have been completed in the year.

English Heritage's obligations under finance leases (note 27) are secured by the lessor's title to the leased assets, which have a carrying value of £11,272,000 (2011: £11,626,000) within land and buildings excluding dwellings. All other property, plant & equipment is owned outright by English Heritage (2011: all).

Notes to the Financial Statements

18 Property, Plant & Equipment

	Operational Land & Buildings £'000	Dwellings £'000	Plant & Machinery £'000	IT £'000	Furniture & Fittings £'000	Assets under Construction £'000	Total £'000
English Heritage and HBMCE							
Cost or Valuation							
At 1 April 2010	59,249	2,318	8,042	4,155	4,067	4,319	**82,150**
Additions	-	-	305	40	134	4,892	**5,371**
Disposals	(9)	-	-	(268)	(23)	-	**(300)**
Impairments	(470)	(82)	-	(26)	-	-	**(578)**
Reclassifications	2,183	-	17	1,226	282	(3,708)	**-**
Revaluations	5,239	1,921	(7)	(413)	-	-	**6,740**
At 31 March 2011	**66,192**	**4,157**	**8,357**	**4,714**	**4,460**	**5,503**	**93,383**
Depreciation							
At 1 April 2010	12,666	842	4,698	2,794	1,837	-	22,837
Charged in year	2,637	53	924	568	638	-	4,820
Disposals	(8)	-	-	(268)	(23)	-	(299)
Revaluations	3,555	(26)	(11)	(280)	-	-	3,238
At 31 March 2011	**18,850**	**869**	**5,611**	**2,814**	**2,452**	**-**	**30,596**
Carrying amount at 31 March 2010	46,583	1,476	3,344	1,361	2,230	4,319	**59,313**
Carrying amount at 31 March 2011	**47,342**	**3,288**	**2,746**	**1,900**	**2,008**	**5,503**	**62,787**
Asset financing:							
Owned	35,716	3,288	2,746	1,900	2,008	5,503	**51,161**
Finance Leased	11,626	-	-	-	-	-	**11,626**
Carrying amount at 31 March 2011	**47,342**	**3,288**	**2,746**	**1,900**	**2,008**	**5,503**	**62,787**

Notes to the Financial Statements

19 Heritage Assets

	Land & Buildings £'000	Artefacts & Archives £'000	Total £'000
English Heritage and HBMCE			
Cost or Valuation			
At 1 April 2011	17,298	6,010	**23,308**
Additions	20	201	**221**
Donations	-	10	**10**
Impairments	(20)	-	**(20)**
Reclassifications	(916)	-	**(916)**
Indexation	(52)	-	**(52)**
Carrying amount at 31 March 2012	16,330	6,221	**22,551**

	Land & Buildings £'000	Artefacts & Archives £'000	Total £'000
English Heritage and HBMCE			
Cost or Valuation			
At 1 April 2010	12,123	5,733	**17,856**
Additions	-	277	**277**
Impairments	(660)	-	**(660)**
Revaluations	5,835	-	**5,835**
Carrying amount at 31 March 2011	17,298	6,010	**23,308**

The table below provides a summary of transactions relating to heritage assets for the current and previous two accounting periods. There are no transactions relating to assets which are not reported in the Statement of Financial Position.

	2012 £'000	2011 £'000	2010 £'000
Cost of acquisition	**221**	277	253
Value acquired by donation	**10**	-	-
Impairments recognised	**(20)**	(660)	(23)

All land and buildings are subject to a full professional valuation every five years. The most recent valuation was undertaken as at 31 March 2011 (note 1i).

All artefacts and archives acquired since 2001 are recognised and held at cost or, where donated, at market value (note 1j).

ENGLISH HERITAGE ANNUAL REPORT AND ACCOUNTS 2011/12

Notes to the Financial Statements

20 Further Information on English Heritage's Heritage Assets

Land and Buildings - Pure Heritage Assets

English Heritage manages the National Heritage Collection of over 400 historic properties throughout England providing a diverse portfolio that includes World Heritage Sites, industrial monuments, castles, historic houses, abbeys, forts, stone circles and a large part of Hadrian's Wall. They range from prehistoric ruins to the lavishly furnished Osborne House. In age they range from Neolithic burial chambers dating from 3500-2600BC to twentieth century houses.

All of the land and buildings at these properties have been classified as either pure heritage (non-operational heritage), operational heritage or operational (non-heritage), (notes 1i and 1j). Over 550 discrete pure heritage assets have been identified and encompass the vast majority of what would be recognised as the main buildings at these properties.

The National Heritage Collection is held by English Heritage under various arrangements, with many being in the guardianship of the Secretary of State for Culture, Olympics, Media and Sport with the freehold being retained by the owner.

The remaining properties are in the ownership of English Heritage, other government departments or the Crown Estate.

Of the pure heritage assets held by English Heritage, only Apethorpe Hall and Harmondsworth Barn (acquired post 1 April 2001) have been capitalised and recognised on the Statement of Financial Position.

During 2011/12, English Heritage purchased Harmondsworth Barn in Middlesex for a total consideration of £20,000 including legal costs (2010: no purchases or donations). This has subsequently been impaired to nil following a valuation undertaken by Powis Hughes as at 31 March 2012. All expenditure on the conservation and maintenance of property has been charged to the Statement of Comprehensive Net Expenditure as it was incurred.

A full listing of the National Heritage Collection is contained in The English Heritage Members' and Visitors' Handbook which is available on the English Heritage website. The handbook also includes full details of public access to these sites.

Land and Buildings - Operational Heritage Assets

English Heritage holds 80 operational heritage assets. None of the acquisitions of land and buildings as disclosed in note 19 relate to operational heritage assets. All expenditure on the conservation and maintenance of property has been charged to the Statement of Comprehensive Net Expenditure as it was incurred.

Historic Artefacts

As part of the National Heritage Collection, English Heritage possesses in the region of 500,000 historic artefacts, ranging from environmental remains and archaeological artefacts, to pottery, fine art and furnishings. They are an integral part of our historic properties. As well as being of significance in their own right, they assist in interpreting and presenting our properties to the public and they provide a valuable research resource for heritage professionals and our own staff.

These collections were formed by the past owners of historic houses and castles or by archaeologists excavating sites and by curators recovering former contents. They come from many sources: some were transferred from the Department of the Environment on 1 April 1984, some from the Greater London Council in 1986, some have been donated, some are the results of archaeological excavations on our properties and others have been purchased as part of our ongoing work to restore and enhance our properties.

Total expenditure of £248,000 was incurred on historic artefacts (including replicas) during the year ended 31 March 2012 (2011: £294,000). £201,000 of this expenditure was charged to Heritage Assets (2011: £277,000) and £47,000 was charged to the Statement of Comprehensive Net Expenditure (2011: £17,000). Donated artefacts received during the year had a value of £10,000 (2011: nil). There were no disposals of artefacts during the year.

Notes to the Financial Statements

20 Further Information on English Heritage's Heritage Assets

A detailed report on the state of English Heritage's collection was completed in 2010, the culmination of 8 years work by the Curatorial Team. This report identified approximately 17,000 items of international significance, 58,000 of national significance with the remaining artefacts being of regional significance.

Of the Historic Artefacts in English Heritage's care, 55% relate to archaeology (which includes all excavated material and documentary records); 30% relate to books and archives (all library and archive holdings at sites and stores, excluding the National Monuments Record archive); 9% relate to decorative arts (items such as replica carpets and curtains, tapestries, stained glass, stone and wood carvings); 4% relate to social and industrial history (items such as arms and armour, coins, machinery and tools); 1% relate to natural history (items such as taxidermy, shells and non-archaeological skeletal material); 0.9% relate to fine art (items such as paintings, sculptures and works of art on paper) and 0.1% relate to ethnography (cultural material such as ritual objects and costumes).

The majority of English Heritage's collection (87%) is kept for research and display value in 44 store locations.

Archives

English Heritage's extensive archives comprise maps, plans, photographs, files, reports and books. The English Heritage Archive holds almost 12 million historic and modern photographs, texts and documents, and is the national record of England's historic environment. Our archives are used by members of the public, professional researchers, other heritage organisations and our own staff. These records have been created by national institutions concerned with national survey programmes and projects, or acquired by them from others. Chief amongst these institutions are: Ordnance Survey Archaeological Record; the former National Buildings Record; the Department of the Environment Library of Air Photography; and the archives and information created by the former Royal Commission on the Historical Monuments of England (RCHME).

No expenditure on acquisition of archives was incurred during the year ended 31 March 2012 (2011: nil). No donated archives received during the year had a value (2011: nil). There were no disposals of archives during the year (2011: nil).

Within the archive, two collections have been acquired post 1 April 2001 and capitalised. The Images of England collection was a project to photograph every listed building in England. It was completed in 2008 and comprises 320,000 photographs. The Oblique Aerofilm collection was acquired in 2008 and contains 1,400,000 oblique aerial images. No other items within the archive are recognised on the Statement of Financial Position.

Of the archive, 79% of items are photographic (including postcards); 5% are drawings, plans or graphical material; 2% are reports and files; 2% are digital materials and 12% are miscellaneous. The archive is arranged by collection. Photographic collections of note include: Aerofilms; Images of England; The RAF Collection (vertical aerial photography from the 1940's onwards); Ordnance Survey; Bedford Lemere and Co (pioneering architectural photography); The John Gay, Eric de Mare and Henry Taunt Collections and the English Courtauld Collection.

Notes to the Financial Statements

21 Conservation and Management

The National Collections Group within English Heritage is responsible for the conservation and maintenance of the English Heritage estate, artefacts and archives. The Estates Team within the Conservation Department is responsible for the historic estate, and the Curatorial Department for artefacts and archives.

Staff caring for the historic estate are split into three teams: Conservation Maintenance, National Projects and Programme Development. Their work is currently divided into three main streams: the Annual Maintenance Programme (planned cyclical and response maintenance); the Minor Planned Maintenance Programme (small repair projects of usually less than £50,000); and the Major Planned Repair Programme (larger long term or one off conservation projects usually of more than £50,000). The team also contribute and provide Project Management resources to the Capital Investment Programme. The work streams are developed in line with the strategy and process set out in the English Heritage Asset Management Plan (AMP). The AMP enables the conservation of the estate to be managed according to nationally-established conservation priorities, give English Heritage an awareness of the scale of the 'conservation deficit' in relation to the resources available to address it along with impact assessments of English Heritage's ability to procure the necessary works. Total expenditure on site maintenance of £13,880,000 was incurred during the year ended 31 March 2012 (2011: £11,613,000). Further information is provided in the separate publication 'Conservation Principles, Policies and Guidance', which is available on the English Heritage website. This sets out the framework within which English Heritage manages its own historic estate as well as the thinking that guides its advice to others. From 2012 the Conservation Department will be split to create a free standing Estates Department within the National Collections Group.

Artefacts are conserved and managed by three teams within the Curatorial Department. The Collections Curatorial Team manages the acquisition and storage of English Heritage's collections and historic interiors. The Collections Conservation Team manages the conservation of historic interiors and collections via its specialists in the care of fine and applied art, conservation science, environmental and pest control and objects care. The Property Curators ensure that the conservation, commercial and visitor led development of English Heritage sites is guided, planned and executed so as to sustain the values and significance of the sites in question. The team are also involved in the development of presentation and interpretation schemes and the development of Heritage Protection agreements at English Heritage sites.

The English Heritage Archive, formerly the National Monuments Record, is maintained within the Curatorial Department of the National Collections Group. The Archive's repository and main public service activities are based in Swindon, Wiltshire. The Archive is a recognised place of deposit under the Public Records legislation and has high environmental standards for the storage of photographs and other archives. The Archive aims to devise and maintain services which reflect varied requirements of a wide range of users. The Archive works closely with the parallel National Monument Records in Scotland and Wales on a range of archives and access projects, and operates in a UK, European and international context especially for common standards on the management of records of the historic environment. The Archive Team ensures the conservation of the collections and archives held by the Archive, and in supporting intellectual and physical access to them by users. Activities include conservation, cataloguing, contributing to access initiatives and maintaining flowlines to ensure that records are deposited with the Archive and made available.

Notes to the Financial Statements

22 Financial Assets

a) HBMCE

	Total £'000
Subsidiary Undertakings	
At 1 April 2010, 1 April 2011 and 31 March 2012	**2,028**

Details of the subsidiary undertakings are given in note 37.

b) English Heritage	2012 £'000	2011 £'000	2010 £'000
Market Value at 1 April	**448**	427	316
Net Investment Gains/(Losses)	**(8)**	21	111
Transfer to Assets Classified as Held for Sale	**(440)**	-	-
Market Value at 31 March	**-**	448	427
Historical Cost	**434**	434	434

At 31 March 2012 the financial assets were held in a single Common Investment Fund managed by M&G Securities Limited and comprised 38,576 units in Charifund. The market value shown is net of investment management fees, 0.4625% p.a. of the value in Charifund.

On 28 March 2012 the Trustee of the Iveagh Bequest agreed that the charities' investments be sold and spent on the Kenwood House Project. These investments are hence disclosed as held for sale.

23 Assets Classified as Held for Sale

English Heritage and HBMCE have the following assets classified as held for sale:

	English Heritage			HBMCE		
	2012 £'000	2011 £'000	2010 £'000	2012 £'000	2011 £'000	2010 £'000
Land and Buildings	392	-	-	392	-	-
Financial Assets	440	-	-	-	-	-
	832	-	-	**392**	-	-

The land and buildings classified as held for sale at 31 March 2012 are Blackfriars Inn in Gloucestershire and the Post Office Cottage and Mount Pleasant Cottage, both at Wroxeter Roman City. The assets are held at the lower of their carrying amount and fair value less costs to sell. No assets were classified as held for sale as at 31 March 2011 or 31 March 2010. At the year end, contracts had been exchanged with a third party for Blackfriars Inn, although the sale did not complete until 2 April 2012. No gain/loss has been recognised in the Consolidated Statement of Comprehensive Net Expenditure.

Notes to the Financial Statements

24 Inventories

	English Heritage			HBMCE		
	2012 £'000	2011 £'000	2010 £'000	**2012 £'000**	2011 £'000	2010 £'000
Inventories	**3,269**	2,959	2,522	**-**	66	46

Inventories are stated after write offs in the year of £104,000 (2011: £148,000) and provisions of £108,000 (2011: £119,000) in English Heritage.

25 Trade and Other Receivables

	English Heritage			HBMCE		
	2012 £'000	2011 £'000	2010 £'000	**2012 £'000**	2011 £'000	2010 £'000
Trade Receivables	**887**	976	1,693	**887**	976	1,693
Value Added Tax	**4,169**	2,474	2,058	**4,169**	2,474	2,058
Prepayments and Accrued Income	**4,656**	6,685	8,475	**4,656**	6,685	8,475
Other Receivables	**1,271**	1,085	2,367	**1,271**	1,085	2,367
Amount Owed by Subsidiary Undertaking	**-**	-	-	**1,263**	942	277
Total Trade and Other Receivables	**10,983**	11,220	14,593	**12,246**	12,162	14,870
Intra-Government Balances						
Balances with Central Government Bodies	**5,152**	3,838	2,533	**5,152**	3,838	2,533
Balances with Local Authorities	**1,185**	184	-	**1,185**	184	-
Balances with Public Corporations	**2**	-	4	**2**	-	4
Balances with Bodies External to Government	**4,644**	7,198	12,056	**5,907**	8,140	12,333
Total Trade and Other Receivables	**10,983**	11,220	14,593	**12,246**	12,162	14,870

Notes to the Financial Statements

26 Financial Instruments

As English Heritage has a Funding Agreement with the Department for Culture, Media and Sport, co-signed by the Department for Communities and Local Government and the Department for Environment, Food and Rural Affairs, it is not exposed to the degree of financial risk normally faced by business entities. Financial instruments play a much more limited role in creating or changing risk than would be typical of the listed companies to which International Financial Reporting Standard (IFRS) 7 mainly applies. English Heritage has no powers to borrow and its only investments are Non-Current Asset Investments related to the Iveagh Bequest held in Common Investment Funds. Surplus funds are held on short term fixed interest rate deposit with institutions with low risk credit ratings, classified as cash and cash equivalents.

As allowed by IFRS 7, receivables and payables that are due to mature or become payable within 12 months from the Statement of Financial Position date have not been disclosed as financial instruments.

a) Liquidity Risk

Owing to the nature of its funding and pattern of expenditure, English Heritage does not have any significant liquidity risk.

b) Interest Rate Risk

English Heritage's long term financial liabilities relate solely to provisions (note 30), none of which are interest bearing and are mainly due within 1 year. The only disclosable financial assets are cash and cash equivalents, current and non-current asset investments which are not exposed to significant interest rate risk.

c) Currency Risk

All financial assets and liabilities are held in sterling.

d) Valuation

There is no material difference between the carrying values and fair values of financial assets and liabilities.

e) Financial Assets

Financial assets consist of cash including fixed asset investments held in a Common Investment Fund (note 22b).

No financial assets classified as fixed term deposits were held at 31 March 2012 (2011: nil).

Notes to the Financial Statements

27 Obligations Under Finance Leases

Total future minimum lease payments under finance leases are given in the table below for each of the following periods:

English Heritage and HBMCE	2012 £'000	2011 £'000	2010 £'000
Obligations under finance leases for the following periods comprise:			
Land & Buildings			
Not Later than One Year	566	566	566
Later than One Year and not Later than Five Years	2,266	2,266	2,266
Later than Five Years	23,222	23,788	24,354
	26,054	26,620	27,186
Less Interest Element	(18,601)	(19,151)	(19,701)
Present Value of Obligations	**7,453**	7,469	7,485

Contingent rents are calculated as the increases in rental costs as a result of rent reviews. During the year £281,000 of contingent rents have been paid (2011 and 2010: £281,000). It is English Heritage's policy to lease certain of its property, plant and equipment under finance leases. The Engine House Building and English Heritage Archive facility lease transfers the risks and rewards of ownership to English Heritage. The assets have been capitalised and are subject to the same revaluation policies as other property, plant and equipment, and are depreciated over the shorter of useful economic life or the lease period with the outstanding lease obligations (net of interest) shown in payables. English Heritage's finance lease policy is disclosed in note 1p.

Net lease liabilities repayable within one year were £566,000 (2011 and 2010: £566,000), in the second to fifth years inclusive £1,878,000 (2011 and 2010: £1,878,000) and after five years £5,009,000 (2011: £5,025,000 and 2010: £5,041,000).

English Heritage's obligations under finance leases are secured by the lessor's rights over the leased asset disclosed above.

Notes to the Financial Statements

28 Trade and Other Payables

	English Heritage			HBMCE		
	2012 £'000	Restated 2011 £'000	Restated 2010 £'000	2012 £'000	Restated 2011 £'000	Restated 2010 £'000
Trade Payables	12,912	8,899	13,017	12,912	8,899	13,017
Income Tax and Social Security	75	1,399	1,442	75	1,399	1,442
Pensions	18	18	18	18	18	18
Deferred Income	8,975	8,080	6,945	8,534	7,711	6,281
Capital Government Grant in Aid	-	340	340	-	340	340
Accruals	14,381	14,206	10,554	14,373	14,206	10,548
Other Payables	843	1,966	2,444	843	1,962	2,441
Total Trade and Other Payables	**37,204**	34,908	34,760	**36,755**	34,535	34,087
Intra-Government Balances						
Balances with Central Government Bodies	1,068	2,620	1,988	1,068	2,620	1,988
Balances with Local Authorities	144	88	424	144	88	424
Balances with Public Corporations	1	1	83	1	1	83
Balances with Bodies External to Government	35,991	32,199	32,265	35,542	31,826	31,592
Total Trade and Other Payables	**37,204**	34,908	34,760	**36,755**	34,535	34,087

29 Other Payables

	English Heritage			HBMCE		
	2012 £'000	Restated 2011 £'000	Restated 2010 £'000	2012 £'000	Restated 2011 £'000	Restated 2010 £'000
Pensions	212	208	237	212	208	237
Deferred Income	2,938	2,873	2,780	2,908	2,822	2,780
Other Payables	**3,150**	3,081	3,017	**3,120**	3,030	3,017

Notes to the Financial Statements

30 Provisions

	Modernisation, Relocation and Restructuring Costs £'000	Legal and Constructive Obligations £'000	Total £'000
Balance at 1 April 2011	6,753	294	7,047
Provided in the Year	19	69	88
Provisions Released in the Year	(22)	(111)	(133)
Provisions Utilised in the Year	(4,942)	-	(4,942)
Balance at 31 March 2012	**1,808**	**252**	**2,060**
Balance at 1 April 2010	3,677	569	4,246
Provided in the Year	4,602	459	5,061
Provisions Released in the Year	(165)	(706)	(871)
Provisions Utilised in the Year	(1,361)	(28)	(1,389)
Balance at 31 March 2011	**6,753**	**294**	**7,047**

A provision of £1,808,000 (2011: £2,293,000 and 2010: £1,648,000) has been made with relation to early retirement costs payable until pensionable age of 60. These are payable by monthly instalments to pensioners until 2019. Provisions are calculated based on third party information provided by pension scheme administrators.

No provision is required in respect of redundancy costs as a result of restructuring at English Heritage (2011: £4,460,000 and 2010: £2,029,000).

A provision of £203,000 (2011: £263,000 and 2010: £474,000) has been made against dilapidations, rent reviews and contractual disputes, with payment likely to be incurred during 2012. The provision has been calculated based on third party information provided by landlords and subcontractors.

A provision of £49,000 (2011: £31,000 and 2010: £95,000) has been made with relation to personal injury and other claims made against English Heritage. The provision has been calculated based on the claim amount and likelihood of payment. Payment is likely to be incurred in 2012.

Notes to the Financial Statements

31 Analysis of Reserves

	2012		2011	
	General Reserve £'000	Revaluation Reserve £'000	General Reserve £'000	Revaluation Reserve £'000
English Heritage and HBMCE				
Balance at 1 April	33,255	23,804	36,300	15,484
Grant in Aid Received	121,193	-	129,854	-
Net Expenditure for the Financial Year	(118,727)	-	(134,397)	-
Other Income	3,284	-	1,046	-
Revaluation	346	1,533	52	8,720
Reserve Transfer	861	(861)	400	(400)
Balance at 31 March	**40,212**	24,476	33,255	23,804

32 Development and Restricted Funds

English Heritage and HBMCE	Balance at 1 April 2011 £'000	Income £'000	Revenue Expenditure £'000	Capital Expenditure £'000	Balance at 31 March 2012 £'000
Kenwood House	298	3	-	-	301
Down House and Gardens	1,396	14	(350)	-	1,060
Eltham Palace	1,257	12	(755)	-	514
Rangers House (Wernher Foundation)	655	6	(6)	(161)	494
Ditherington Flax Mill	39	1	-	(40)	-
Wrest Park	1,446	13	-	(1,459)	-
London Squares	14	-	-	(14)	-
Total Restricted Funds	5,105	49	(1,111)	(1,674)	2,369
Development Fund	2,746	287	-	(380)	2,653
Total Funds	7,851	336	(1,111)	(2,054)	**5,022**

	2012 £'000	2011 £'000
The Total Funds were held as pooled investments as follows:		
Cash and Cash Equivalents	**5,022**	7,851

Notes to the Financial Statements

33 Cash and Cash Equivalents

English Heritage	2012 £'000	2011 £'000	2010 £'000
Balance at 1 April	16,332	13,914	15,360
Net change in Cash and Cash Equivalents Balances	(2,539)	2,418	(1,446)
Balance at 31 March	**13,793**	16,332	13,914

The following balances at 31 March were held with:

Cash

Government Banking Service	276	-	-
Commercial Banks	13,517	6,332	3,914
	13,793	6,332	3,914

Cash Equivalents

Commercial Banks	-	10,000	10,000
Balance at 31 March	**13,793**	16,332	13,914

HBMCE	2012 £'000	2011 £'000	2010 £'000
Balance at 1 April	15,831	13,412	14,860
Net change in Cash and Cash Equivalents Balances	(2,539)	2,419	(1,448)
Balance at 31 March	**13,292**	15,831	13,412

The following balances at 31 March were held with:

Cash

Government Banking Service	276	-	-
Commercial Banks	13,016	6,331	3,912
	13,292	6,331	3,912

Cash Equivalents

Commercial Banks	-	9,500	9,500
Balance at 31 March	**13,292**	15,831	13,412

ENGLISH HERITAGE ANNUAL REPORT AND ACCOUNTS 2011/12

Notes to the Financial Statements

34 Commitments

a) Grant Offers Made to Other Bodies and Individuals

	Total £'000
Commitment Outstanding at 1 April 2011	57,075
Grants Paid During the Year	(31,375)
New Grant Offers Made During the Year Net of Lapsed Offers	34,931
Commitment Outstanding at 31 March 2012	**60,631**

b) Contracts

Expenditure contracted for as at 31 March 2012 but not provided for in the financial statements amounted to £25,027,000 (2011: £12,581,000) including capital commitments of £3,634,000 (2011: £3,691,000), of which £3,634,000 (2011: £3,207,000) related to tangible non-current assets and nil (2011: £484,000) related to intangible non-current assets.

c) Operating Leases

Total future minimum lease payments under operating leases are given in the table below for each of the following periods, split between land and buildings and other.

	2012 £'000	2011 £'000
Land and Buildings		
Not Later than One Year	2,443	2,626
Later than One Year and not Later than Five Years	8,451	7,488
Later than Five Years	19,354	11,489
	30,248	21,603
Other		
Not Later than One Year	95	159
Later than One Year and not Later than Five Years	34	75
Total Operating Lease Commitments	**30,377**	21,837

The majority of leases relate to property rentals and are subject to rent reviews. During the year ended 31 March 2012 payments under operating leases totalled £4,123,000 (2011: £3,333,000).

35 Losses and Special Payments

	2012 £'000	2011 £'000
Losses	200	309
Special Payments	26	78
Total Losses and Special Payments	**226**	387

Notes to the Financial Statements

36 Contingent Liabilities

Various outstanding claims existed at 31 March 2012. Provision has been made in the accounts for the year ended 31 March 2012 for those outstanding liabilities which will probably require settlement by English Heritage and where the amount of the liability can be reliably estimated (note 30). No other contingent liabilities have been identified at 31 March 2012 (2011: contingent liabilities estimated not to exceed £250,000).

37 Subsidiary Undertakings

a) English Heritage Trading Limited

HBMCE is the sole shareholder of English Heritage Trading Limited, incorporated in 1994.

The following results of English Heritage Trading Limited have been included in the consolidated results:

Income and Expenditure	2012 £'000	2011 £'000
Turnover	14,632	14,068
Expenditure	(13,622)	(12,890)
Operating Profit	1,010	1,178
Interest Receivable and Similar Income	5	5
Profit on Ordinary Activities Before Gift Aid	1,015	1,183
Gift Aid to HBMCE	(1,015)	(1,183)
Profit on Ordinary Activities Before and After Taxation	-	-

Net Assets as at 31 March	2012 £'000	2011 £'000
Current Assets	3,770	3,394
Creditors: Amounts Falling Due Within One Year	(1,712)	(1,315)
Creditors: Amounts Falling Due After More Than One Year	(30)	(51)
Net Assets	2,028	2,028
Share Capital - Ordinary Shares at £1 Each	2,028	2,028
Profit and Loss Account	-	-
Shareholder's Funds	2,028	2,028

b) English Heritage Limited

HBMCE is the sole guarantor of English Heritage Limited, a company limited by guarantee incorporated in 1984. English Heritage Limited was dormant throughout the current and prior years.

Notes to the Financial Statements

c) The Iveagh Bequest

The Commissioners of English Heritage are also the Trustee of the Iveagh Bequest, a Trust established in 1929 by the Iveagh Bequest (Kenwood) Act for the benefit of Kenwood House. In 1997 Statutory Instrument No 482 transferred Custodian Trusteeship to English Heritage.

The Iveagh Bequest's principal place of business is 1 Waterhouse Square, 138-142 Holborn, London, EC1N 2ST.

On 28 March 2012, the Trustee of the Iveagh Bequest agreed that the charity's investments be sold and be spent on the Kenwood House project. These investments are hence disclosed as current asset investments.

The following results of the Iveagh Bequest have been included in the consolidated results:

Statement of Financial Activities	2012 £'000	2011 £'000
Incoming Resources		
Investment Income: Dividends Receivable	22	22
Resources Expended		
Charitable Expenditure: Distributions to HBMCE	(22)	(22)
	-	-
Net Outgoing Resources		
Gain/(Loss) on the Revaluation of Investment Assets: Unrealised Gain/(Loss)	(8)	21
Net Movement in Funds	(8)	21
Fund Balances Brought Forward 1 April	448	427
Fund Balances Carried Forward 31 March	**440**	448
Net Assets as at 31 March		
Non-Current Asset Investments	-	448
Current Asset Investments	440	-
Net Assets	**440**	448
Capital Fund Reserves	**440**	448

38 Landfill Tax Credit Scheme

English Heritage is registered as an Environmental Body with "Entrust", the regulator of environmental bodies under the landfill tax regulations. During the year ended 31 March 2012 there were no projects in progress that were grant funded by landfill tax credits (2011: none).

39 Post Balance Sheet Event

There were no post balance sheets events.

Donors, Sponsors and Contributors

English Heritage is very grateful to all the benefactors, charitable trusts and grant-making organisations that have contributed to or sponsored its activities during the year ended 31 March 2012. The following have given amounts of, or worth, £1,000 or more:

Individual Donations
Mr Adam Abrahams
Mrs Appleby
Mrs Ann Broder
Mrs O J Coombe
Ms Rachel Darnley-Smith
Ms Joyce Drakard
Mrs Verna Evans
Miss Janian Foy
Mr Richard Hunting
Mr Stefan Kossoff
Lord Lloyd-Webber
Mrs N P Moore
Ms Cora Newell
Mr Simon Palley
Mrs Iris Perry
Mr Donald Smalley

Grant Making & Public Bodies
Arts Council England
Cadw
Construction Industry Training Board
The Crown Estate
Department for the Environment, Food and Rural Affairs
Doncaster Metropolitan Borough Council
European Union
HASSRA
Heritage Lottery Fund
Lantra
National Heritage Training Group
Natural Environment Research Council
Newcastle City Council
Rural Payments Agency
South West Regional Development Agency

Legacies
Mr Robert J Dickinson
Ms Beryl Double
Mr David Efemey
Miss Dorothy Grice
Miss Margaret Halstead
Mr Ronald Handley
Mrs Mary Kiddle
Ms Wendy Olga Marriott
Mrs Joan Miller
Mrs Barbara Hilary Lymn Murdoch
Mr Ronald Nunn
Mr Arthur Owen

Charitable Trusts
The ACE Foundation
The Atlas Fund
Chiswick House Friends
English Heritage Foundation
Foyle Foundation
Friends of Audley End
The Friends of the Iveagh Bequest, Kenwood
Icon
Island Friends of Royal Osborne
John Laing Charitable Trust
The John S Cohen Foundation
Kenwood Dairy Restoration Trust
National Trust
The Steel Charitable Trust
The Wolfson Foundation

Corporate Partners & Support
Customworks Ltd
David Austin Roses Ltd
Ecclesiastical Insurance Group plc
The Great British Card Company
John Lewis Partnership plc
Johnson Matthey plc
Land Securities plc
Little Greene Paint Company Ltd
Network Rail Ltd
Royal Mail Group Ltd
Universal Pictures International UK & Eire Ltd
Welspun UK Ltd

We have received significant support from the English Heritage Foundation (charity no 1140351). We would like to thank its donors and trustees for the projects they have made possible this year, including those at Wroxeter Roman Fort and the Royal Artilliary Monument.

In addition to the donors, sponsors, legators and contributors listed above, during the year ended 31 March 2012 we also received pledges of future support from many other organisations and individuals and we look forward to acknowledging them all in our Annual Report and Accounts in future years.

We also thank those not listed here – together their gifts constitute a significant sum – as well as all donors who prefer to remain anonymous.